SMARTGUIDE

CREATIVE
HOMEOWNER®

D0473708

perennials
& bulbs

CREATIVE HOMEOWNER®, Upper Saddle River, New Jersey

COPYRIGHT © 2009

CRE·TIVE
HOMEOWNER®

A Division of Federal Marketing Corp.
Upper Saddle River, NJ

SMART GUIDE: PERENNIALS & BULBS

TECHNICAL EDITOR	Miranda Smith
GRAPHIC DESIGNER	Kathryn Wityk
JUNIOR EDITOR	Jennifer Calvert
PHOTO COORDINATOR	Robyn Poplasky
INDEXER	Schroeder Indexing Services
DIGITAL IMAGING SPECIALIST	Frank Dyer
FRONT COVER PHOTOGRAPHY	Jerry Pavia

CREATIVE HOMEOWNER

VICE PRESIDENT AND PUBLISHER	Timothy O. Bakke
ART DIRECTOR	David Geer
MANAGING EDITOR	Fran J. Donegan

Current Printing (last digit)
10 9 8 7 6 5 4 3

Manufactured in the United States of America

Smart Guide: Perennials & Bulbs, First Edition
Library of Congress Control Number: 2008921444
ISBN-10: 1-58011-420-2
ISBN-13: 978-1-58011-420-2

CREATIVE HOMEOWNER®
A Division of Federal Marketing Corp.
24 Park Way
Upper Saddle River, NJ 07458
www.creativehomeowner.com

Metric Conversion

Length

1 inch	25.4 mm
1 foot	0.3048 m
1 yard	0.9144 m
1 mile	1.61 km

Area

1 square inch	645 mm²
1 square foot	0.0929 m²
1 square yard	0.8361 m²
1 acre	4046.86 m²
1 square mile	2.59 km²

Volume

1 cubic inch	16.3870 cm³
1 cubic foot	0.03 m³
1 cubic yard	0.77 m³

Common Lumber Equivalents
Sizes: Metric cross sections are so close to their U.S. sizes, as noted below, that for most purposes they may be considered equivalents.

Dimensional lumber	1 x 2	19 x 38 mm
	1 x 4	19 x 89 mm
	2 x 2	38 x 38 mm
	2 x 4	38 x 89 mm
	2 x 6	38 x 140 mm
	2 x 8	38 x 184 mm
	2 x 10	38 x 235 mm
	2 x 12	38 x 286 mm
Sheet sizes	4 x 8 ft.	1200 x 2400 mm
	4 x 10 ft.	1200 x 3000 mm
Sheet thicknesses	¼ in.	6 mm
	⅜ in.	9 mm
	½ in.	12 mm
	¾ in.	19 mm
Stud/joist spacing	16 in. o.c.	400 mm o.c.
	24 in. o.c.	600 mm o.c.

Capacity

1 fluid ounce	29.57 mL
1 pint	473.18 mL
1 quart	1.14 L
1 gallon	3.79 L

Weight

1 ounce	28.35g
1 pound	0.45kg

Temperature
Celsius = Fahrenheit – 32 x ⅝
Fahrenheit = Celsius x 1.8 + 32

contents

safety first

All projects and procedures in this book have been reviewed for safety; still it is not possible to overstate the importance of working carefully. What follows are reminders for plant care and project safety. Always use common sense.

- *Always* use caution, care, and good judgment when following the procedures in this book.

- *Always* determine locations of underground utility lines before you dig, and then avoid them by a safe distance. Buried lines may be for gas, electricity, communications, or water. Contact local utility companies who will help you map their lines.

- *Always* read and heed tool manufacturer instructions.

- *Always* ensure that the electrical setup is safe; be sure that no circuit is overloaded and that all power tools and electrical outlets are properly grounded and protected by a ground-fault circuit interrupter (GCFI). Do not use power tools in wet locations.

- *Always* wear eye protection when using chemicals, sawing wood, pruning trees and shrubs, using power tools, and striking metal onto metal or concrete.

- *Always* consider nontoxic and least toxic methods of addressing unwanted plants, plant pests, and plant diseases before resorting to toxic methods. Follow package application and safety instructions carefully.

- *Always* read labels on chemicals, solvents, and other products; provide ventilation; heed warnings.

- *Always* wear a hard hat when working in situations with potential for injury from falling tree limbs.

- *Always* wear appropriate gloves in situations in which your hands could be injured by rough surfaces, sharp edges, thorns, or poisonous plants.

- *Always* protect yourself against ticks, which can carry Lyme disease. Wear light-colored, long-sleeved shirts and pants. Inspect yourself for ticks after every session in the garden.

- *Always* wear a disposable face mask or a special filtering respirator when creating sawdust or working with toxic gardening substances.

- *Always* keep your hands and other body parts away from the business end of blades, cutters, and bits.

- *Always* obtain approval from local building officials before undertaking construction of permanent structures.

- *Never* employ herbicides, pesticides, or toxic chemicals unless you have determined with certainty that they were developed for the specific problem you hope to remedy.

- *Never* allow bystanders to approach work areas where they might by injured by workers or work-site hazards. Make sure all work sites are well marked.

- *Never* work with power tools when you are tired, or under the influence of alcohol or drugs.

- *Never* carry sharp or pointed tools, such as knives or saws, in your pocket.

Perennial and Bulb Gardens

Smart Guide: Perennials & Bulbs will help you create attractive gardens, borders, and other plantings using perennials and bulbs. Perennials and many bulbs grow back each season, providing recurring colors and textures that can serve to anchor your landscape. You can plant them separately for an eye-catching display or use them in combination to enjoy extended blooming times. Smart gardeners team perennials and bulbs with annuals to vary their garden designs from year to year. No matter which course you take, you can use this book to design a well-planned garden that will reflect your creativity and personal tastes.

Smart Guide: Perennials & Bulbs guides you through the basics of gardening. You'll learn how to select the best plants for your location and which plants will thrive under ideal and not so ideal conditions. Handy guides will tell you when popular perennials and bulbs are at their best. Extensive directories of favorites provide important information about the plants, including sizes, planting requirements, maintenance recommendations, and the best cultivars of each variety. And because they appear year after year, there is information on planting, transplanting, and dividing these plants.

about perennials

Planning

A perennial is a plant that lives for at least three years. The plants we think of as perennials are, for the most part, herbaceous, meaning that aboveground parts of the plant—the stems and leaves—are soft and green, not woody. In cold climates the top growth of most herbaceous perennials dies back each winter and the plants become dormant; in spring, new top growth develops. In warm climates, some perennials are evergreen, retaining their leaves and stems all year; others become dormant during summer droughts.

Using Perennials

Perennials are flower garden classics. You can grow them in beds and borders by themselves, in combination with annuals and bulbs, or with small shrubs, trees, and ground covers.

The majority of perennials are most valued for their lovely flowers, though many produce attractive foliage. The art of garden design is partially a matter of combining plants with various blossom colors, textures, and shapes. With perennials—as opposed to annuals that bloom all season—time also becomes an important design element. Because most perennials bloom for just a few weeks a season, you'll need to choose plants that bloom at differing times to have garden color throughout the season.

Many perennials spend most of the growing season as a clump of stems and leaves, so good design also depends on choosing plants for their overall form, texture, and foliage. In fact, experienced garden designers treat plant form, texture, and foliage as the primary design qualities, and flower color as a secondary consideration. See pages 8–9 for examples of some of the most common plant and flower forms and page 12 for foliage qualities.

Choosing Plants. As you begin to choose perennials, make a list of plants that you've seen and liked in

Add interest to your garden by combining plants with a variety of sizes, forms, and flower types, as well as a pleasing mix of colors.

An artful contrast of plant forms is achieved here by placing geraniums, aloe, and snakeplant in front of yucca.

other gardens, books, and nursery catalogs. For each one, note the flower color and form, its time of bloom, the height and shape of the plant, and its foliage shape and color. This may sound like a lot of work, but it makes things much easier when you lay out your garden. To help narrow down your list, weed out all the plants that aren't suited to your growing conditions—temperatures, light, soil, and moisture.

If making this list seems daunting, rest assured that many a good garden has come into being through a process of trial and error. Don't be intimidated. After all, if you don't like a perennial in one spot, you can always dig it up and move it next year.

Plants grow in a number of forms, or *growth habits*. Combining plants with a variety of growth habits adds interest to any planting. Choose from the following when planning your beds and borders:

Mounded—rounded and bushy, mounded plants form a cushion of foliage, usually close to the ground. Examples include bergenia (left) and lady's mantle (*Alchemilla*, right).

Branching—branching plants grow upright, with branched stems that give them an open appearance. Examples include false spirea (*Astilbe* species, left) and asters (right).

Upright—some plants are decidedly vertical with a narrow, upright form. Blazing star (*Liatris spicata*, left) and irises (right) are common upright plants.

Trailing or matlike—some plants stay low to the ground because they sprawl. Perennials that fit this category include these garden pinks (*Dianthus species*, top), and creeping phlox (*Phlox subulata*, bottom).

Seasonal Stars

Most perennials bloom for just two to three weeks a year, so if you want to have flowers blooming throughout the growing season, you'll need to combine plants with different bloom times. For a long display, interplant spring and summer-blooming bulbs and annuals, many of which flower all summer long, with your perennials.

Orchestrating a succession of bloom from spring to fall can be a complicated job. To make it easier, first make a map of the garden-to-be. Draw in the locations of clumps of plants before you decide what they will be. After that, choose your color scheme and assign colors to the different plant clumps.

Now it's time to select plants. Choose those in the appropriate colors, being mindful to plan for a variety of blooming times, heights, plant forms, flower shapes, and textures. Use the box on pages 10–11 to guide you to perennials that flower at different times. (See pages 20–69 for profiles of these plants.)

Flower Forms

To make your garden more exciting, include flowers in a variety of shapes. Since many flowers are spherical, include some of the following:

Cup-shaped or bell-shaped flowers, such as those of tulips and this bellflower, look like upward-facing cups or dangling bells.

Trumpet flowers, exemplified by day-lilies and lilies, as illustrated above, have a narrow, tubular throat and widely flared, pointed petals.

Spiky flowers are often clusters of small blooms growing along a vertical stem. Speedwells (*Veronica* species) and salvias, as illustrated above, are good examples of spiky flowers.

Daisylike flowers, such as tickseed and this boltonia, have round centers surrounded by lots of narrow petals. These blooms are actually composed of disc flowers that make up the center, and ray flowers (which often look like petals) that circle the central disc flowers.

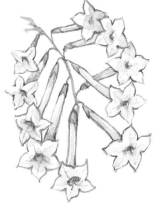

Tubular flowers are elongated and sometimes flare at the top. They are more narrow and slender than trumpets. Good examples are foxglove (*Digitalis* species) and this nicotiana.

Blooming Season

Spring-blooming Perennials:
- Bergenia (*Bergenia* species)
- Bleeding heart (*Dicentra spectabilis*)
- Candytuft (*Iberis sempervirens*)
- Christmas rose (*Helleborus niger*)
- Cranesbill (*Geranium* species)
- Columbine (*Aquilegia* species)
- Foxglove (*Digitalis purpurea*)
- Garden pinks (*Dianthus* species)
- Goatsbeard (*Aruncus dioicus*)
- Iceland poppy (*Papaver nudicaule*)
- Iris (*Iris* species and cultivars)
- Lady's mantle (*Alchemilla* species)
- Lenten rose (*Helleborus orientalis*)
- Oriental poppy (*Papaver orientale*)
- Peony (*Paeonia* species)
- Primrose (*Primula* species)
- Red-hot poker (*Kniphofia uvaria*)
- Salvia (*Salvia* species)
- Sweet violet (*Viola odorata*)
- Thrift (*Armeria maritima*)

Summer Perennials:
- Baby's breath (*Gypsophila paniculata*)
- Balloon flower (*Platycodon grandiflorus*)
- Beard-tongue (*Penstemon* species)
- Bee balm (*Monarda didyma*)
- Bellflower (*Campanula species*)
- Blanket flower (*Gaillardia* X *grandiflora*)
- Blazing star (*Liatris spicata*)
- Butterfly weed (*Asclepias tuberosa*)

- Cardinal flower (*Lobelia cardinalis*)
- Catmint (*Nepeta* X *faassenii*)
- Coneflower (*Rudbeckia* species)
- Cranesbill (*Geranium* species)
- Daylily (*Hemerocallis* cultivars)
- Delphinium (*Delphinium* species)
- False indigo (*Baptisia australis*)
- False spirea (*Astilbe* species)
- Fringed bleeding heart (*Dicentra eximia*)
- Garden phlox (*Phlox paniculata*)
- Garden pinks (*Dianthus* species)
- Great blue lobelia (*Lobelia siphilitica*)
- Lavender (*Lavandula* species)
- Ligularia (*Ligularia* species)
- Meadowsweet (*Filipendula* species)
- Monkshood (*Aconitum* species)
- Obedient plant (*Physostegia virginiana*)
- Pincushion flower (*Scabiosa caucasica*)
- Plantain lily (*Hosta* species)
- Purple coneflower (*Echinacea purpurea*)
- Red-hot poker (*Kniphofia uvaria*)
- Rose mallow (*Hibiscus moscheutos*)
- Russian sage (*Perovskia atriplicifolia*)
- Salvia (*Salvia* species)
- Showy primrose (*Oenothera speciosa*)
- Speedwell (*Veronica* species)
- Sundrops (*Oenothera fruticosa*)
- Thrift (*Armeria maritima*)
- Tickseed (*Coreopsis* species)
- Tufted pansy (*Viola cornuta*)
- Yarrow (*Achillea* species)

Late Summer and Fall Perennials:
- Aster (Aster species)
- Autumn Joy stonecrop (Sedum 'Autumn Joy')
- Blazing star (Liatris species)
- Boltonia (Boltonia asteroides)
- Bugbane (Cimicifuga species)
- Coneflower (Rudbeckia species)
- Garden chrysanthemum (Chrysanthemum X grandiflorum)
- Goldenrod (Solidago cultivars)
- Monkshood (Aconitum species)
- Obedient plant (Physostegia virginiana)

Bleeding heart

Tickseed

Blazing star

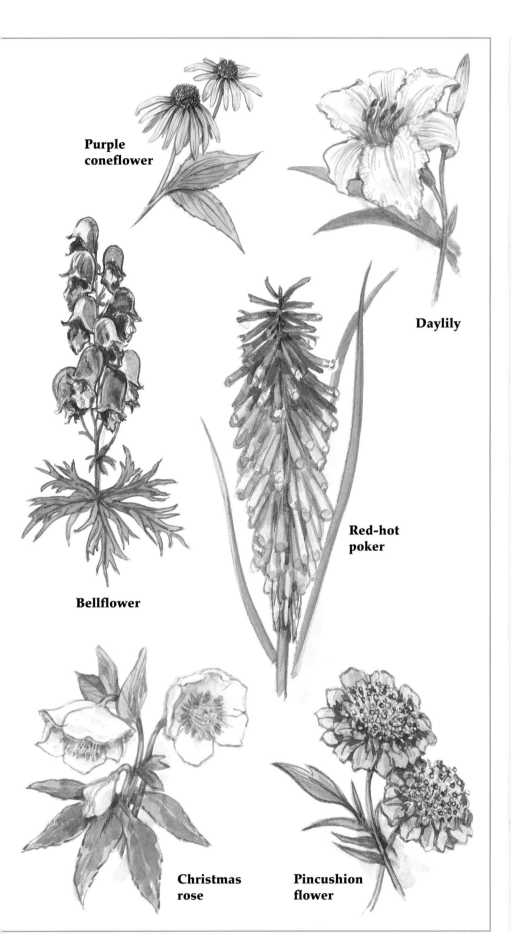

Purple coneflower

Daylily

Bellflower

Red-hot poker

Christmas rose

Pincushion flower

Long-Blooming Perennials

Some perennials bloom for an especially long time. They are beautiful in themselves but are also valuable because they help bridge gaps between more seasonal flowers that come and go. The following plants bloom continuously for four to six weeks, or produce flushes of bloom off and on all summer. Some plants, such as foxgloves and some delphiniums, often bloom a second time if cut back after flowering.

- 'Autumn Joy' stonecrop (*Sedum* 'Autumn Joy')
- Balloon flower (*Platycodon grandiflorus*)
- Bee balm (*Monarda didyma*)
- Blanket flower (*Gaillardia* species)
- Bugbane (*Cimicifuga racemosa*)
- Catmint (*Nepeta* X *faassenii*)
- Coneflower (*Rudbeckia fulgida* 'Goldsturm')
- Daylily (*Hemerocallis* 'Stella de Oro', 'Black Eyed Stella', and 'Happy Returns')
- Fringed bleeding heart (*Dicentra eximia*)
- Lancaster geranium (*Geranium sanguineum* var. *striatum*)
- Obedient plant (*Physostegia virginiana*)
- Purple coneflower (*Echinacea purpurea*)
- Speedwell (*Veronica spicata* 'Goodness Grows' and 'Sunny Border Blue')
- Thrift (*Armeria maritima*)
- Tickseed (*Coreopsis verticillata* 'Moonbeam')
- Yarrow (*Achillea* species)

Flowers come and go in a perennial garden, but from spring until fall the leaves are always there. One secret of great garden design is to choose plants for their foliage as well as their flowers. Here are some guidelines to get you started.

A variety of leaf sizes and textures adds interest. Big, bold leaves such as those of bergenia or hosta bring substance and drama to a composition. Delicate, feathery leaves such as those of yarrows, fringed bleeding heart, and threadleaf coreopsis look airy and light. Spiky, upright foliage like that of irises contributes vertical lines that add drama to a collection of low or mounded plants.

Different shades of green add complexity to a bed or border. Combine blue-green, gray-green, yellow-green, deep forest green, and light spring green for more appeal. Lighter greens can bring an area forward visually or light up a shady spot while darker greens can make areas recede. Once you begin to notice foliage colors, you'll appreciate their subtleties.

Colored foliage can add excitement or help soften bright colors. Chartreuse and golden leaves such as those of some hostas can light up a dim corner of the garden. Purple-red leaves, such as those of *'Husker Red'* penstemon (*P. digitalis*) are dramatic. Silver foliage such as that of artemisias helps blend strong colors (especially in sunny gardens) and softens harsh contrasts; it imparts a feeling of misty softness to a more subdued garden of blue and pink flowers.

Variegated leaves, patterned with two or more colors, can add dimension. They may be edged, streaked, striped, splashed, spotted, flushed, or mottled with two, three, or even more colors. Use a light hand when adding variegated plants—too many make plantings look busy and chaotic, and can actually detract from the flowers.

chapter 2
growing perennials

Basic Care

Growing perennials successfully is easy and straightforward. You'll have to plant them well and then take care of them by fertilizing, pinching and pruning as necessary, preparing them for winter, and dividing them when they get crowded.

When you order plants from a nursery catalog, you may receive them planted in a pot. Or they may be dormant and in "bare-root" form, with their roots surrounded by a moist packing material and then wrapped in plastic or other material. Planting techniques are different for each type of plant.

A symphony of color from easy-to-grow plants, this garden includes Shasta daisies, columbines, campanula, and delphiniums.

Planting Bare-root Perennials

1. Transplant bare-root plants in early spring, while they are still dormant. When the plants arrive, unpack them right away and examine them. The roots and crowns should be firm, with no mold or soft spots. Shoots should be woody and only a couple of inches long—new green growth means the plant is no longer dormant, and thus more susceptible to damage from cold weather or frost.

2. Set the plants in a bucket, and soak the roots overnight or for several hours. Dig the planting holes before you remove the plants from the bucket. Fill the holes with water, and let them drain. Follow the nursery's directions for planting depth—it's important for the plants' long-term health. Most plants thrive if the crown is level with the soil surface, but there are exceptions.

3. Make a mound of soil in the bottom of the hole, and set the plant on top, gently spreading the roots out over the mound. If the roots are too few or too short to cover a mound, just spread them out in the bottom of the hole. Work soil around and between the roots with your fingers. When the hole is half filled with soil, water again. When the water drains away, fill the hole the rest of the way with soil.

4. Firm the soil around the base of the plant, and water again. If necessary, add more soil to level the surface. Water to keep the soil consistently moist for a few weeks as the plants settle in. If you're planting in the spring, make a berm around the planting hole to retain irrigation water. If planting in the fall, mulch the plant once the top inch of the ground is frozen.

Give plants enough space to develop to their full mature size. Crowded plants don't grow as well or flower as profusely and are more prone to disease. These plants will fill in the space as they grow.

This plant is root-bound from being in the nursery container for too long.

Planting Container Plants

When choosing plants at a local garden center or nursery, look for sturdy, stocky plants with good color. Young, compact plants will be less likely to suffer transplant shock than older, bigger plants that are already in bloom. Avoid plants that look spindly, lanky, or pale; also avoid those with torn or broken leaves, signs of insect or disease damage, or moss growing on the soil.

When you buy perennials in pots at a local outlet, ask the staff if the plants were field-grown or container-grown. If the plants were grown in the field and just potted up for sale, treat them like bare-root plants, and get them into the ground as soon as you can. With container-grown plants, you have a few more options.

Timing. Container-grown plants can be transplanted whenever the weather is not too stressful. It's best to plant when you can count on rain and moderate temperatures for a few weeks, so spring is a good planting time in most climates. Fall is also favorable except in Zones 5 and cooler because it can cool too quickly. Where the heat is not too intense and the weather is not too dry, you can also plant in summer.

If you can't transplant right away, water and set your plants in a shady spot as soon as you get them home. When you're ready to plant, first decide exactly where they will go. Set the pots out on top of the soil surface to refine your arrangement. Once you're satisfied with the design, dig the planting holes before proceeding.

Remove the plant from the pot. Place your fingers around the stem, and hold the edges of the pot or soil with one hand while you turn over the pot with your other hand. Let the plant slide out of its pot. If the plant sticks, tap the bottom of the pot with a trowel handle, or slide a knife blade vertically around the inside of the pot to separate the root ball from it. Once it's out of the pot, gently squeeze the root ball to loosen and separate the roots a bit, then set the plant in its hole, keeping the soil ball as intact as you can.

Set the plant at the same depth it was growing in its pot. Fill the hole, working the soil in around the root ball with your fingers. Water well; then add more soil if necessary to fill the hole to the top.

Maintaining Perennials

Although perennials remain in the garden year after year once planted, they do need some regular mainte-nance in order to continue looking their best. Most perennials benefit from watering during dry spells and periodic fertilizing. Some plants bene-fit from having their stems pinched back when they are young to encour-age bushier growth. Many bloom longer if you deadhead them. Most perennials need to be dug up and their root clumps divided periodically to keep them vigorous. It's also a good idea to cut back the stems of perennials as they die back for the winter. Not only does this give you a neat looking garden all winter, it also removes some hiding places for pests and plant diseases. Finally, in climates where the ground freezes in winter, a good mulch can protect perennial roots from suffering dam-age during the cold months.

If you find roots at the bottom of the root ball that are tightly coiled around and around in the shape of the pot, you've unwittingly purchased a root-bound (or pot-bound) plant. Simply putting the plant in the ground may not solve the problem—the roots may continue to grow in a circle, even in the garden (a condition known as "container habit"). A plant with container habit won't send new roots out into the soil. It can survive only as long as you give it regular doses of water and fertilizer, and only if the soil does not freeze to the depth of the root ball in winter.

Here are some ways to help a root-bound plant:

With a heavy-duty screwdriver, pry loose some of the largest, toughest roots in the center of the root mass. Pull them out and cut them off.

Gently untangle and spread out some of the roots.

If the plant has a taproot, straighten it out as much as you can without breaking it.

With a sharp knife, make 2 or 3 vertical cuts up into the root ball from the bottom. Gently spread the roots when you set the plant in the hole.

Cut off any roots growing on top of the soil or wrapped around the plant's stem.

Fertilize new plants after you transplant them. Spread the fertilizer around the plants, and scratch it into the soil.

Fertilizing Perennials. All perennial garden areas benefit from a top-dressing of compost or aged manure in early spring to maintain the soil's organic matter content and make better use of any fertilizers you apply, whether synthetic or organic.

If you use organic fertilizers, add them to the soil when you first prepare it or when you set out new plants. You can also top-dress with compost two or three times during the growing season or apply liquid fertilizers such as seaweed products and fish emulsion as foliar feeds, spraying them onto the leaves as plants grow. Follow package directions for dilution and application rates, and spray only before the sun is up or on cloudy (but not rainy) days.

If you use synthetic fertilizers, apply them when you transplant or when established plants begin to grow in spring. Thereafter, in sandy, poor to moderately fertile soils, fertilize every four to six weeks at half the rate recommended on the label. In heavier soils with marginal fertility, fertilize every six to eight weeks. In good soil, fertilize every two months or so at half-strength if it is sandy, but every eight to ten weeks if it is heavy. No matter what your soil type, stop fertilizing six weeks before the average date of the first fall frost in your area.

Cut back perennials at the end of the growing season. These Siberian irises are ready for cutting back in fall, when the leaves begin to yellow.

Fall Cleanup. At the end of the growing season, it's time to clean up the garden and prepare it for winter. In cold climates, cut back all the herbaceous plants in fall, to 3 to 4 inches from the ground. Wait until early spring to cut back shrubby plants such as lavender; fall pruning could induce these plants to send out new growth that would in all likelihood be damaged by winter cold. In warm climates, cut back spring and summer bloomers in autumn, but wait until they finish flowering to trim later bloomers. No matter where you live, fall is a good time to remove stakes and clean up any weeds or debris that have found their way into the garden.

Winter Mulches. After the soil freezes at least an inch deep, spread a winter mulch of evergreen boughs or a 6- to 8-inch layer of loose straw or shredded leaves throughout the garden. This mulch protects the dormant roots because it prevents winter sunlight from warming the underlying soil, keeping it more consistently frozen. When the soil experiences repeated cycles of freezing, thawing, and refreezing over the course of the winter, it can warp and buckle. This action can tear roots or heave (push) them right out of the ground. Thus exposed, the roots can be damaged or killed by cold temperatures and drying winter winds.

This Siberian iris plant desperately needs division—it has a bare hole in the center with good growth around it.

Dividing Perennials

As perennials grow year after year, most of them expand, forming ever-larger clumps of roots. After a number of years, as the clump of roots becomes crowded and the older central portions grow woody, the plants tend to grow less vigorously and flower less lavishly. You may even notice that the stems appear to grow in a ring, with none growing up from the central part of the crown. When this happens, it's time to give the plants a new lease on life by dividing them. Division is also a great way to increase your stock of plants, because what was one plant becomes two, three, or even five new ones. How often plants need to be divided varies widely; chrysanthemums need to be divided every year or two, while peonies can remain in place for decades without needing division.

If you live where autumn weather is cool and frost comes early, it's best to divide your perennials in spring. But in Zones 6 and warmer, you can divide in early to midfall. (In unseasonably warm years, Zone 5 gardeners can divide fast-growing plants in fall.) Transplant early enough so the divided plants have several weeks to send out new roots and establish themselves in the soil before it freezes.

1. To minimize plant stress, divide and transplant on a cloudy day. Unless it has rained recently, water the plants well two or three days beforehand. Cut back stems by about one-third. This decreases water loss and eases transplant shock.

2. On moving day, first dig holes for the new transplants. Then loosen the roots by digging around the outside of the clump. Dig straight down until you are below the root ball, then angle under the plant. Push back and forth to loosen the plant; then lift it out of the soil.

3. Shake off loose soil; divide the plant into sections with both roots and growth buds. Pull apart loose clumps with your fingers, but use a sharp knife to cut apart dense clumps.

4. When dividing a number of plants, keep a pail of water or a wet towel handy to soak or wrap up divisions until you get them replanted. Discard the old, woody central parts of the clump; replant only the firm, young, outer portions. Before replanting, check the roots and prune any broken or straggly ones.

5. Water the planting hole; set in the plant; and fill around it with soil so it's at the same depth. Water, but don't fertilize for a few weeks.

6. Label the transplants so you'll know what you planted where.

Achillea

Achillea species
Yarrow

These perennials are grown for their flat-topped, tight clusters of tiny white, pink, yellow, red, cream, and burnt-orange flowers. Most species grow tall with fernlike foliage which is toothed or divided. The leaves are aromatic when crushed, and some yarrows are grown in herb gardens for their healing properties.

Blooming Time: Midsummer; until fall for some cultivars if deadheaded regularly.

Hardiness: Zones 3 to 10.

Height: 1½ to 4 feet, depending on species.

Spacing: 1½ feet.

Light: Full sun.

Soil: Well-drained, average fertility.

Moisture: Average; tolerates some drought.

Garden Uses: Grow yarrow in the middle to the back of beds and borders. The golden yellow cultivars are lovely with blue and violet flowers, and the pale yellow 'Moonshine' is especially versatile. Yarrows are good cut flowers.

Comments: Yarrows tolerate hot, dry conditions and do well in dry, exposed locations.

Recommended Cultivars:
• 'Coronation Gold', to 3 ft.; deep golden yellow
• *A. filipendulina* 'Gold Plate', to 4 ft.; golden yellow

'Summer Pastels'

• *A. millefolium*, to 3 ft.; 'Cerise Queen', rose pink; 'Lilac Beauty', lilac; 'Red Beauty', crimson
 A. 'Moonshine', to 2 ft.; light lemon yellow
• *A. ptarmica* 'The Pearl', 1½–2 ft.; double round white flower heads
• Galaxy Series, hybrids of *A.* 'Taygetea' and *A. millefolium*, salmon, pink, yellow.

Drying Yarrow

Yarrow air-dries beautifully. Gather cut stems in bunches with rubber bands and hang upside down in a dry, airy place.

SMART TIP

Cutting Yarrow for the Vase
For cut flowers, gather yarrow stems when about half the florets in the cluster have opened, and before any pollen is evident. The foliage is also attractive in arrangements.

Lady's mantle leaves after a rain

Alchemilla

Alchemilla mollys
(formerly *A. vulgaris*)
Lady's mantle

These low, mounded plants are grown primarily for their rounded, lobed, grayish green leaves. The combination of plant habit and color make lady's mantles decorative all through the season. In late spring they produce airy clusters of small chartreuse flowers on slender, branched stems.

Blooming Time: Late spring to early summer.

Hardiness: Zones 3 to 9.

Height: 10 inches to 1½ feet.

Spacing: 1 to 1½ feet.

Light: Full sun in cool climates, partial shade elsewhere.

Soil: Well-drained, average fertility.

Moisture: Average to even.

Garden Uses: Grow lady's mantle as an edging or in the front of a bed or border. They look good with almost every color and make a good filler plant, both in the garden and in the vase.

Comments: These small plants have a charming ability to hold glistening drops of rain or dew on their leaves. They form low, spreading clumps and may self-sow. Lady's mantle grows best where summers are not too terribly hot.

Recommended Cultivars: No cultivars are commonly available.

SMART TIP

Volunteer Lady's Mantle Plants
Lady's mantle self-seeds easily, as evidenced by the volunteer plants growing in the crevices on the steps. Deadhead the blooms before they set seed to avoid volunteer plants.

The spring blooms of lady's mantle look like a lovely chartreuse green froth rising above the leaves.

McKana Giant hybrid columbines

Aquilegia

Aquilegia species
Columbine

Columbines are native to the mountainous regions of the world. Their gracefully spurred blooms are a highlight of many spring flower gardens. A number of species are native to North America, and a host of hybrid cultivars is available in a lovely range of colors. The flowers are carried at the top of slender stalks rising from a low mound of distinctively scalloped leaves. The handsome leaves in combination with the graceful plant habit make columbines attractive all through the season.

Blooming Time: Spring to early summer.

Hardiness: Zones 3 to 10, varies with species.

Height: 1 to 3 feet.

Spacing: 1 to 1½ feet.

Light: Full sun in cooler climates, partial shade elsewhere.

Soil: Well-drained, average fertility.

Moisture: Average.

Garden Uses: Grow columbines in the front to middle ground of beds and borders, in rock gardens, and in cottage gardens.

Comments: Columbines self-sow readily in many gardens and cross freely with one another. For best results, divide or replace with new plants every three or four years. If leaf miners attack, remove and destroy affected leaves at the first sign of tunneling.

Recommended Cultivars:
• 'Blue Butterflies', just over 1 ft.; blue with white edges
• *A. caerulea*: Rocky Mountain columbine, to 2½ ft.; white petals with lavender to blue spurs
• *A. flabellata*: 'Alba', Japanese fan columbine; 1–1½ ft.; white
• Biedermeier Group, 1½ ft.; white-tipped petals, many colors
• 'Hensol Harebell', 2½–3 ft.; deep violet-blue, blooms until midsummer in most areas
• McKana Giant hybrids, to 2½ ft.; light and dark pink, bicolors of red, yellow, blue
• Music hybrids, 1½ ft.; yellow, cream, red-and-white, pink-and-white, blue-and-white, pink-and-yellow, red-and-yellow.

Music strain

SMART TIP

Saving Columbine Seeds
When seed pods are dry and seeds rattle inside them, clip the stems and sprinkle the seeds over the garden where you want new columbines next year.

Thrift

The combination of thrift and catmint is particularly effective with this pebble mulch. Both plants fare well in less-than-ideal soils, making this a good combination for areas with dry or thin soils.

Armeria

Armeria maritima
Thrift, Sea pink

These low-growing plants bear 1-inch-round, pom-pom-shaped clusters of small flowers on tall slender stems. The mounded plants form tufts of grassy, evergreen leaves. The plants remain attractive all season and can double as a ground cover on slopes or in other hard-to-mow locations. They tolerate both salty and dry soils, too.

Blooming Time: Late spring to early summer.

Hardiness: Zones 3 to 10.

Height: 6 inches to slightly over a foot.

Spacing: 8 inches to 1 foot.

Light: Full sun.

Soil: Well-drained, sandy to loamy, average fertility.

Moisture: Average to slightly dry.

Garden Uses: Grow thrift in the front of beds and borders, in seashore gardens, in rock gardens, on slopes, or as edging plants.

Taller varieties are good for cutting, and cut flowers last up to a week in the vase. Cut the flowers when they have just begun to open, and condition them before arranging by standing them in fresh water nearly up to the base of the flower heads for several hours. Thrift's small, round flower heads make good fillers in arrangements of larger daisylike and spiky flowers.

Comments: Deadhead to encourage reblooming. Thrift flowers cut well and add nice form and color to arrangements. Divide plants every few years.

Recommended Cultivars:
- 'Alba', 6 in., white
- 'Ornament', 1 ft., rose pink, white, and deep salmon.

Planting Armeria Seeds

1. Sow the seeds indoors in a container of moist, porous potting medium. Cover with plastic film to retain soil moisture and humidity. Seeds will germinate in approximately 10 days.
2. Thrift seeds need darkness to germinate. Cover the flat with layers of newspaper to block light.

'Powis Castle'

Artemisia

Artemisia species
Artemisia

'Silver King'

Southernwood

Artemisias are a large genus of aromatic plants grown primarily for their foliage. The varied plant habits, leaf forms, and foliage colors make them extremely useful in flower gardens. Artemisias may be low and mounded or tall and upright; the foliage can be cut or lobed, or finely dissected and lacy-looking. Colors range from green through gray-green and silvery white. The plants produce tiny clusters of yellow or white flowers, but most gardeners remove them because the flowers themselves are not particularly attractive and also because they can distract from the overall appearance of the plant.

Hardiness: Zones 4 to 10, depending on species.

Height: 1 to 5 feet, depending on species.

Spacing: 1 to 2 feet.

Light: Full sun.

Soil: Well-drained, sandy, average to poor fertility.

Moisture: Average to occasionally dry.

Garden Uses: An asset in beds and borders, the muted foliage is a good blender for bright-colored flowers and brings a soft, misty feeling to a garden of pink and blue flowers. Plant artemisias in the front, middle, or back of the garden, depending on their height.

Comments: Artemisias are easy to grow. If plants start to look straggly in hot, humid weather, cut them back to stimulate new growth. Artemisias are also easy to dry for use in winter wreaths and arrangements. Dry them by hanging in a dark, airy location. If you plan to use them for a wreath, tie the stems onto a circular form while they are still green and let them dry that way.

Recommended Cultivars:
• *A. abrotanum*: southernwood, to 4 ft.
• *A. schmidtiana*: 'Silver Mound', 1 ft.
• *A.* 'Powis Castle', 2–3 ft.; fine, feathery dissected leaves
• *A. ludoviciana* var. *albula*, 'Silver King', to 3 ft.; silvery white toothed leaves.

Pruning Flower Stalks

Blooms on this 'Silver Mound' artemisia rise above the silvery gray foliage, giving a ragged look to what was a tidy mound of delicate leaves. It's easy to prune them off to retain the plant's good looks.

Aruncus

Aruncus dioicus
Goatsbeard

Goatsbeards are bushy, shrubby plants with toothed, compound, rough-textured leaves. Their feathery clusters of tiny white flowers are similar to those of astilbe. Goatsbeard is an American native, hailing from eastern North America.

Goatsbeard plants are either male or female. Both kinds bloom, but the flowers of female plants are more drooping and a slightly greenish white color. Flowers of male plants are creamy white with prominent stamens.

Blooming Time: Late spring to early summer.

Hardiness: Zones 3 to 9.

Height: 4 to 6 feet.

Spacing: 3 feet.

Light: Full sun to partial shade; in warmer climates, provide some shade, especially in the afternoon.

Soil: Fertile, humusy.

Moisture: Even to abundant.

Garden Uses: Goatsbeard makes a good background or screening plant; it can take the place of a shrub in summer borders. It is also a great plant for a woodland garden.

Goatsbeard flowers are good for cutting, too, and can be dried as well. Cut the flowers when they are just begin-

Goatsbeard

ning to open, early in the morning if possible. Condition them before arranging by immediately placing them in a container of water filled to just below the base of the flower heads. Leave the stems in the deep water for several hours. Then strip off all the leaves that would be underwater in the vase, and recut the stems when you arrange the flowers in a vase.

If you wish to dry goatsbeard, use silica gel rather than air-drying the flowers. The flowers dry quickly, so check them frequently after the first few days to prevent them from becoming brittle.

Comments: After several years, if flowering declines and plants look less vigorous, divide them in early spring while still dormant.

Recommended Cultivars: 'Kneiffii' grows only to 3 ft.

Dividing Goatsbeard Plants

1. When goatsbeard plants become crowded, dig the clumps and divide them. Grasp near the base of the stem and pull or cut the root clump into sections.

2. Make certain that each section contains both roots and stems. Cut back the stems for easier handling, before or after digging. Replant the divisions, and water well.

Asclepias

Asclepias tuberosa
Butterfly weed

Like other milkweeds, butterfly weeds grow in clumps of sturdy upright stems lined with narrow oblong leaves. Butterfly weeds are smaller than many milkweeds. In summer they produce many dense clusters of bright orange, yellow-orange, or red-orange flowers that attract butterflies.

Blooming time: Mid- to late summer.

Hardiness: Zones 3 to 10.

Height: 1½ to 2½ feet.

Spacing: 6 inches to 1 foot.

Light: Full sun.

Soil: Well-drained, sandy or coarse-textured, average fertility.

Moisture: Average to low; tolerates drought when established.

Garden Uses: Plant butterfly weed near the front of an informal garden, especially one designed to attract butterflies.

Comments: Butterfly weed must have good drainage; it will not thrive or even survive long in wet conditions. Start new plants from seed; the tuberous roots do not like to be disturbed. Mulch roots over the winter in Zones 3 to 6 to protect them from heaving.

Recommended Cultivars: Gay Butterflies mixture is a mix of red, orange, and yellow shades.

Butterfly weed

Butterfly on butterfly weed

SMART TIP

Saving Butterfly Weed Seeds
Asclepias seeds blow away in the slightest wind when they are mature. To keep them, use a rubber band to tie a paper bag over the seed stalks when they begin to turn brown. When the pods split, the seeds will fall into the bag.

Aster

Aster species
Michaelmas daisy

The best perennial asters for gardens belong to three different species: *A* x *frikartii*, Frikart's aster; *A. novae-angliae*, New England aster; and *A. novi-belgii*, New York aster. All produce daisylike flowers with many narrow petals or ray flowers around a central disk. Plants bloom in shades of purple, blue, pink, and red, as well as white. Asters are upright and branching, and their somewhat sparse foliage can sometimes make them a bit weedy looking.

Blooming Time: Late summer into autumn.

Hardiness: Zones 4 to 8, depending on cultivar.

Height: 1 to 4 feet.

Spacing: 1 to 2 feet.

Light: Full sun.

Soil: Well-drained, average fertility.

Moisture: Evenly moist.

Garden Uses: Plant asters in the middle or back of beds and borders, depending on height.

Comments: For best bloom, divide asters every two or three years in the early spring. Discard the old, woody central parts of the crowns, and replant the vigorous outer sections. Stake plants as they grow. Pinch back the stems to keep them more compact and encourage flowering.

New England aster

Recommended Cultivars: *A.* x *frikartii*:
- 'Wonder of Staffa', to 2½ ft.' lavender-blue
- 'Mönch', 2–2½ ft.; light lilac-blue

A. novae-angliae:
- 'Alma Pötschke', 3 ft.; rose pink
- 'Harrington's Pink', 4 ft.; clear pink
- 'September Ruby', 3½ ft.; deep crimson

A. novi-belgii:
- 'Audrey', 15 in.; lavender-blue
- 'Boningale White', 3½ ft.; white, double
- 'Crimson Brocade', 3 ft.; crimson
- 'Patricia Ballard', 2 ft.; deep pink
- 'Professor Kippenburg', 1 ft.; light blue
- 'Coombe Violet', 2 ft.; blue-purple

Attracting Butterflies

Butterflies need late season food sources as much as they need the early and midseason bloomers. Asters make a pretty display while also providing an excellent source of nectar.

'Mönch'

'Coombe Violet'

'Purple Lance'

Astilbe

Astilbe species
False spirea

These lovely, feathery perennial garden favorites, sometimes (incorrectly) called spireas, are native to China and Japan. Astilbes are noted for their tall, airy panicles of tiny fluffy flowers that arise from a mass of glossy green, toothed foliage.

Blooming Time: Early to midsummer.

Hardiness: Zones 4 to 8.

Height: 1 to 4 feet.

Spacing: 10 inches to 2 feet.

Light: Partial shade; full sun may burn the foliage and bleach out the flower colors.

Soil: Fertile, rich in organic matter.

Moisture: Abundant.

Garden Uses: Use astilbes in the perennial border or mass them in damp, shady spots. Place the dwarf cultivars in the front of beds and borders or use them as an edging. Astilbes make good cut flowers and can also be dried for winter bouquets. For fresh arrangements, cut flower heads when they are just beginning to open. If possible, cut in the morning or early evening. As soon as you cut them, plunge the stems into a container of cool water up to the base of the flowers. Let the flowers stand in the water for several hours, then remove the leaves, recut and split the stem ends, and immediately arrange the flowers.
 Dry astilbe blossoms in silica gel—they usually shrink and lose their form when air-dried.

Comments: Propagate astilbes by division in spring or fall. In zones 7 and warmer, astilbes may not live long. You can often prolong their lifespan as well as keep them healthier if you provide them with at least 1½ inches of water (3 gallons per square foot of root area) each week.

Recommended Cultivars:
• hybrids of *A.* x *arendsii*, bloom in early summer; shades of pink, rose, red, white
A. chinensis:
• 'Fanal', 1–1½ ft.; blooms in midsummer; light pink
• 'Pumila', to 1 ft.; mid- to late summer; raspberry pink
A. chinensis var. *taquetii,* 3–4 ft.; dense, upright panicles:
• 'Superba', rosy purple
• 'Purple Lance', deep rosy purple
• *A. simplicifolia* 'Sprite', to 1 ft.; pink

Dividing Astilbe Plants

1. Astilbes respond well to division. Dig crowded clumps in spring or fall. Cut clumps into sections with a sharp shovel.
2. Drive the shovel blade completely through the root clump. Then prune out the old woody parts, and replant the younger divisions.

'Fanal'

Baptisia

Baptisia australis
Blue false indigo

This perennial grows into a clump of stems that looks something like a bush. Given its height and width, it can pinch-hit for a narrow shrub in the summer garden. It bears attractive oval, gray-green, three-part leaves on its upright stems. The spikes of striking violet-blue flowers resemble those of lupines or peas, and the individual flowers are formed like those of peas and beans. Flowers are followed by pealike pods that rattle when dry.

Blooming Time: Early summer.

Hardiness: Zones 3 to 9.

Height: 3 to 5 feet.

Spacing: 2 to 3 feet.

Light: Full sun to partial shade; some shade is beneficial in warm climates.

Soil: Well-drained, mildly acid.

Moisture: Average; tolerates some drought but does not tolerate wet soil.

Garden Uses: Grow blue false indigo in place of a small shrub in a mixed bed or border, in the back of the perennial garden, or in a row to make a summertime hedge. Both the flowers and seedpods are good for cutting; the seedpods make a lovely addition to fall and winter bouquets.

Comments: Attractive when in bloom and pleasantly green the rest of the season, false indigo is easy to grow as long as you can give it well-drained soil. Don't deadhead if you want to use the seedpods in dried arrangements or retain them for late-season interest in the fall garden.

Recommended Cultivars: No cultivars are commonly available, although there are two white-flowered Baptisia species—*B. alba* and *B. lactea*. The flowers of B. alba hang down, and the blooms of both species may be marked with blue streaks.

Blue false indigo

Pealike baptisia flowers

Cutting Baptisia Pods

Baptisia seedpods are decorative in fresh or dried flower arrangements. Cut stems containing a group of pods.

Bergenia cordifolia 'Perfecta'

Bergenia

Bergenia cordifolia
Heartleaf bergenia

Bergenias send up loose, rounded clusters of pink flowers at the top of upright stems that rise from clumps of thick, rounded, glossy green, cabbage-shaped leaves. The leaves turn coppery bronze to reddish in fall.

Blooming Time: Early spring.

Hardiness: Zones 3 to 9.

Height: 1 to 1½ feet.

Spacing: 1 foot.

Light: Full sun to partial shade; some afternoon shade is beneficial in warm climates.

Soil: Well-drained, humusy, but tolerates a range of soils and pH.

Moisture: Average to moist.

Garden Uses: Bergenia is attractive in the front of the garden, along a sidewalk or path, or under deep-rooted trees or shrubs.

Comments: The plants are usually evergreen in mild climates and semi-evergreen elsewhere. They spread a bit to form clumps. Slugs can be a problem. Propagate by division of crowded clumps.

Recommended Cultivars:
- 'Perfecta', pinkish red flowers
- 'Bressingham Ruby', rosy pink flowers; red winter leaves
- 'Bressingham White', white flowers
- 'Purpurea', deep pink flowers; purple-tinged leaves
- 'Sunningdale', red flowers; red stems; red winter leaves

SMART TIP

Siting Heartleaf Bergenia Plants
Bergenia plants are equally at home in gardens exposed to morning sun (above) as they are in those that are partially shaded for much of the day (below). No matter where you grow them, plant in masses to get the strongest effect.

Milky bellflower

Carpathian harebell, 'Alba'

Clustered bellflower

Campanula

Campanula species
Bellflower, Harebell

Known for their old-fashioned cup- or bell-shaped flowers, bellflowers range from small, low growers for rock gardens to tall, upright species for the middle of beds and borders. Most are erect and branching and have narrow to oblong leaves of medium to deep green.

Blooming Time: Early to late summer

Hardiness: Zones 4 to 8.

Height: 6 inches to 4 feet.

Spacing: 10 inches to 1½ feet.

Light: Full sun to partial shade.

Soil: Average to fertile, well-drained, humusy.

Moisture: Average to moist.

Garden Uses: Plant low-growers as an edging, in the front of beds and borders, or in rock gardens. Use taller species in the middle ground of beds and borders.

Comments: Generally easy to grow. Some taller types need staking. Many will repeat bloom if deadheaded.

Recommended Cultivars: *C. carpatica*, Carpathian harebell: 6–10 in.:
- 'Alba', white
- 'White Clips', white
- 'China Doll', lavender-blue
- 'Blue Clips', blue, midsummer, reblooming till fall
- *C. glomerata*, Clustered bellflower: 2 ft.; blue or white
C. lactiflora, Milky bellflower: 3–4 ft.; blue or white; arching stems with clusters of flowers near the ends:
- 'Loddon Anna', to 4 ft.; light pink
- 'Prichard's Variety', 3–4 ft.; blue-violet
C. persicifolia, Peach-leaved bellflower: 2–3 ft.:
- 'Alba', white
- 'Grandiflora Alba', white
- 'Telham Beauty', lavender-blue.

Transplanting Bellflower Seedlings

1. Transplant perennial campanula seedlings in either the early spring or fall. Leave enough space between the seedlings so they can grow for several years before they need dividing.

2. Mulch the transplanted plants as soon as possible, particularly if you are planting in fall. Mulches keep weeds down during the summer and protect roots from heaving during the cold months.

Chrysanthemum

Chrysanthemum x *grandiflorum*
Garden mum

Chrysanthemums are the undisputed queens of the fall garden and a staple of both the cut-flower garden and gift-plant market. Commercial greenhouses force mums into bloom year-round, but for gardeners, chrysanthemums and autumn are synonymous. Their rich, earthy colors are unbeatable in late summer and fall. There are many, many cultivars available, and a large assortment of plant heights, flower forms, and flower sizes. They are easy to overwinter, but some people treat them as annuals and buy new ones each year.

Blooming Time: Late summer to fall.

Hardiness: Zones 4 to 10.

Height: 1 to 6 feet.

Spacing: 1½ feet.

Light: Full sun is crucial—even a little bit of shade will interfere with performance.

Soil: Rich, very well-drained, light and loose.

Moisture: Even.

Garden Uses: Mums are a classic for late-season beds and borders. When grown as annuals, they make good plants for containers.

'Blanche Poitevene'

'Autumn Kimberly'

'Louisa'

Comments: Start preparing the mum's soil a couple of months or even a season before you intend to plant. Dig plenty of compost, leaf mold, or well-aged manure into the bed, and check the drainage; mums are subject to root rot in wet soils. If your soil is heavy, consider making raised beds for your plants.

'Legend'

'Deanne Joy'

Individual plants bloom for three or four weeks each, but choosing cultivars wi--h different blooming periods can give you chrysanthemum flowers from late summer well into fall, through several frosts.

A few weeks before planting in spring, fertilize the planting area with an all-purpose fertilizer and some superphosphate. If you garden organically, incorporate rock phosphate into the soil when you dig in the compost or manure, and add greensand to the top few inches when you plant.

Start your chrysanthemum bed with plants or rooted cuttings from a nursery. Hybrid cultivars won't come true from seed, and plants from the florist don't often survive in the garden. Spacing distance will vary according to the sizes of the cultivars you are growing.

During the growing season, feed the plants weekly with half-strength fish emulsion or use a commercial timed-release fertilizer twice during the season. Make sure the plants get plenty of moisture, especially during hot summer weather. Keeping plants mulched helps ensure even moisture levels.

Most chrysanthemums need to be pinched back. When the plant is at least 5 inches tall, pinch out the growing tip to force it to branch. Pinch the plant at least once more as it grows, and pinch the tips evenly all over the plant to give it a symmetrical shape. Where the growing season is short, stop pinching in midsummer so that the plants will bloom before the onset of cold weather.

In cold-climate gardens, a good winter mulch is important because the plants are not always entirely hardy. As an alternative to mulching, you can dig up the plants after they bloom and put them in a cold frame for winter.

Recommended Cultivars: The range of cultivars expands each year. Choose according to color, flower form, and plant habit.

'Coral Rynoon'

'Yellow Illusion'

'Pennine Oriel'

Coreopsis

Coreopsis species
Tickseed

The golden yellow, daisylike flowers of coreopsis are a mainstay of the summer flower garden. The plants are branched and bushy. The foliage varies from one species to another; the leaves of some are fine and threadlike, others have toothed, somewhat coarse leaves, and the leaves of some species are narrow and lance shaped.

Blooming Time: Summer.

Hardiness: Zones 3 to 9; varies with species.

Height: 8 inches to 3 feet.

Spacing: 8 inches to 1 foot.

Light: Full sun.

Soil: Any well-drained, average garden soil.

Moisture: Average; avoid damp to wet soil.

Garden Uses: Plant coreopsis in the front to middle of beds and borders or in a cutting garden.

Comments: Deadhead regularly to prolong bloom. Divide established clumps in spring or fall. The plants hold up well in hot weather. Cut flowers can last up to a week.

Recommended Cultivars: *C. grandiflora*, 2 ft.; yellow flowers; does well in warm climates:
• 'Early Sunrise', semidouble; blooms all summer; yellow
• 'Goldfink', 9 in.; yellow flowers
• 'Sunray', 20 in.; double or semidouble yellow flowers

C. lanceolata, Lance-leaved coreopsis; 2 ft.; yellow flowers:
• 'Ruth Kelchen', to 1½ ft.; gold flowers with a brick red "eye"
C. verticillata, Threadleaf coreopsis; to 3 ft.; threadlike leaves:
• 'Moonbeam', 2 ft.; blooms all summer; pale yellow flowers
• 'Grandiflora', golden yellow flowers
• *C. rosea*, 15 in.; pink flowers, threadlike leaves.

'Early Sunrise'

'Moonbeam'

Self-sown seedlings in early spring

Prolonging Bloom Time

Deadhead coreopsis promptly to keep plants blooming. Pick off spent flowers by hand or use flower shears for efficiency.

Delphinium

Delphinium species

Delphiniums are highlights of the summer flower garden for two reasons—the glorious shades of blue in which their flowers bloom, and the sheer size of their flower spikes, which can top out at 6 feet or even more. The vertical flowering stems soar above divided, deep green leaves.

Blooming Time: Summer.

Hardiness: Zones 3 to 7.

Height: 2 to 7 feet, depending on species or cultivar.

Spacing: 1 to 2½ feet.

Light: Full sun.

Soil: Well-drained, fertile, rich in organic matter, and loose to a depth of 2 feet.

Moisture: Constant, even.

Garden Uses: Plant smaller species and dwarf cultivars in the front to the middle of beds and borders, tall hybrids in the back of the garden. Delphiniums are stately, elegant plants for formal gardens and perennial beds and borders. They also make good cut flowers.

Comments: Delphiniums demand ideal growing conditions—rich soil is essential. They prefer cool weather but

'Fancy Diana'

Pacific Coast hybrid

in cold climates are best treated as annuals. Tall stems need staking. The plants are prone to black spot and crown rot. Plants may produce a second, smaller batch of flowers in fall if you remove the faded flower spikes.

Recommended Cultivars: Blackmore and Langdon strain, 4–7 ft.; blue shades, purple, white, cream:
• Pacific Coast hybrids (Round Table series), to 7 ft.
• 'Black Knight', deep violet with a black center
• 'Blue Bird', medium blue with a white center
• 'King Arthur', violet with a white center
• 'Galahad', white
• 'Pennant Mix', 2–2½ ft. dwarf; blues, rose, creamy white
D. x *belladonna*, 5 ft.; easier to grow than other types; light blue, deep blue, white
• 'Bellamosum', 4 ft.; deep blue
• 'Casa Blanca', 5 ft.; white

Saving Delphinium Seeds

1. To save seeds, cut stems when the seed heads are dry and place them in paper bags to dry completely.
2. When the seeds are fully dry, separate the seed from the chaff. Store seeds in air-tight, labeled containers in the freezer.

SMART TIP

Staking Delphiniums
Delphinium flower spikes can be heavy. To prevent their blowing over and to keep the stems straight for cutting, tie them to tall stakes.

'Zing Rose'

'White Joy'

Dianthus

Dianthus species
Garden pinks

The perennial pinks most often found in garden centers—allwood pinks (*Dianthus* x *allwoodii*), cheddar pinks (*D. gratianopolitanus*), and cottage or grass pinks (*D. plumarius*)—bear small disk-shaped flowers on slender upright stems. The petals have fringed or toothed edges. Perennial pinks come in many shades of pink, rose, red, salmon, and white; many are bicolored. The low, mat-forming plants have grassy, gray- or blue-green leaves.

The flowers of sweet William (*Dianthus barbatus*) are gathered into clusters at the top of upright, branched plants 1 to 2 feet high; they bloom in many shades of pink, rose, red, red-violet, and white, often with bands of a lighter or darker shade. The plants are biennial but sometimes behave as perennials.

Blooming time: Late spring to midsummer.

Height: 4 inches to 2 feet.

Spacing: 6 to 12 inches.

Light: Full sun to partial shade; some afternoon shade is helpful where summers are hot.

Soil: Average fertility; light, well-drained, sandy, with neutral to slightly alkaline pH.

Moisture: Some can tolerate drought; most need average moisture.

Garden Uses: Many garden pinks have a delightful, spicy-sweet clove fragrance. Position them in the front of the garden; low forms are especially pretty spilling over the edges of a path.

Comments: Plant with the crowns right at the soil surface; do not plant too deeply. All dianthus species self-seed easily. You'll notice this particularly with sweet Williams; volunteers are likely to grow many feet away from their parents. Dianthus flowers are edible and have a spicy clove-like flavor. They will dye sugar syrups pink if warmed in them. Strain before using.

Recommended Cultivars:
• *D.* x *allwoodii*: Allwood hybrids, 4– 12 in.; bear fragrant flowers in shades of red, rose, pink
• *D. deltoides*: Maiden pinks, 4–12 in.; tolerates partial shade; red, rose, white flowers
• *D. plumarius*: Cottage pinks, 9–18 in.; fragrant white or pink flowers
• 'Bath's Pink', 6–10 in.; tolerates summer heat and humidity well; many small, fragrant, light pink flowers

SMART TIP

Deadheading Dianthus
Deadhead garden pinks to keep plants producing flowers. If you want plants to self-sow, let some flowers mature late in the blooming season. Collect ripe seedpods or let them shatter where they grow.

Digitalis

Digitalis species
Foxglove

Foxgloves' tall spikes of tubular flowers appear above low clumps of oblong leaves. They come in shades of pink, rose, purple, and white, with spotted throats. In ideal conditions, they self-sow readily, forming large colorful patches.

Blooming Time: Late spring to early summer.

Hardiness: Zones 4 to 8.

Height: 2 to 5 feet.

Spacing: 1 to 2 feet.

Light: Partial shade to full sun.

Soil: Well-drained, humusy, fertile.

Moisture: Average to moist.

Garden Uses: Foxgloves make a good vertical accent for the middle or back of beds and borders. They're also good in

Foxgloves are excellent in partially shaded areas.

'Glittering Prizes'

cottage gardens. Because they thrive in partial shade, use them to brighten areas under trees or by a wall.

Comments: Foxgloves are biennials that often self-sow. In rural areas you may see a group that have seeded themselves from plants in a nearby garden. They're likely to grow on the margins of fields or the edges of woods. Cut them back after first flowerimg, and they may rebloom in late summer. All plant parts are poisonous if eaten.

Recommended Cultivars:
- 'Alba', 4 ft.; white flowers
- 'Glittering Prizes', 4 ft.; white, pink, rose
- 'Foxy', 3 ft.; shades of cream, yellow, rose (only cultivar that blooms the first year from seed)
- *D. x mertonensis*, 3 ft.; rich strawberry red blooms
- *D. grandiflora*, related species; perennial growing to 30 in. with light yellow flowers.

Saving Foxglove Seeds

1. Cut the seed stalks when the pods are completely dry but before they have opened.

2. Place the seed stalks in a paper bag as soon as you cut them. The bag will catch seeds that fall from the pods.

3. Remove chaff from the seeds before storing them in a tightly covered and labeled container.

Echinacea

Echinacea purpurea
Purple coneflower

These sturdy, long-blooming plants are known for their purple-pink daisylike flowers with bronzy brown centers. The plants are upright and branched with coarse-textured, narrowly oval leaves. The centers become elongated as they mature and make excellent additions to dried flower arrangements and winter bouquets.

Blooming Time: All summer into autumn.

Hardiness: Zones 3 to 8 or 9.

Height: 2 to 4 feet.

'White Swan'

Spacing: 1½ to 2 feet.

Light: Full sun.

Soil: Well-drained, average to poor fertility.

Moisture: Average to low, tolerates drought.

'Magnus'

Garden Uses: Ideal plants for meadows, low-maintenance gardens, and informal beds and borders, purple coneflowers are also seen in herb gardens because of their use as a popular herbal remedy. The flowers attract butterflies.

Comments: Plants are easy to grow and extremely dependable. The leaves can sometimes be disfigured by powdery mildew; problems are most severe during high humidity and in poor air-circulation conditions. Divide mature plants every three to five years in the spring or fall.

Recommended Cultivars:
- 'Bright Star', 2 ft.; bright rose pink
- 'Magnus', 3½ ft.; deep purple-pink
- 'White Swan', 3 ft.; white.

Saving Purple Coneflower Seeds

1. To save seeds, let echinacea flowers produce seed heads and when fully dry and dark-colored, clip them off.

2. Place the seed heads in a paper bag to let them dry completely. After a week or so, shake the bag to loosen the seeds.

3. Pour the contents of the bag into a bowl; separate the seeds from the chaff; and store the seeds in an air-tight container.

Geranium

Geranium species
Cranesbill

Hardy geraniums, also called cranesbills, are a large genus of perennials. These plants should not be confused with the tender geraniums grown as summer annuals, which belong to the genus Pelargonium. Most cranesbills are relatively low-growing and sprawling, producing open to slightly cup-shaped flowers on slender, branched stems lined with divided leaves. Flowers come in many shades of pink as well as lilac and blue.

Blooming Time: Mid- to late spring into summer; relatively long-blooming.

Hardiness: Zones 4 to 10, but varies with species.

Height: 6 inches to 1½ feet.

Spacing: 8 inches to 1 foot.

Soil: Well-drained, average fertility.

Moisture: Average; most can tolerate some dryness, but not prolonged drought.

Garden Uses: Plant cranesbills in the front of informal beds and borders. Some are suited to rock gardens; low, spreading types can be used for ground covers in the garden.

Comments: Cranesbills are durable, dependable, easy to grow, and charming in informal settings. Dead-heading guarantees their bloom for many weeks. Propagate plants by dividing established clumps in early spring or fall.

Recommended Cultivars:
• *G. cinereum*, 6–8 in.; small pink flowers
• *G. endressii* 'Wargrave Pink', 1–1½ ft.; salmon pink
• 'Johnson's Blue', hybrid growing to 1½ ft.; bright blue flowers through most of summer
• *G. sanguineum*, blood-red cranesbill; 10–12 in.; magenta
• var. *striatum* (Lancaster geranium), 6–8 in.; pink flowers veined in red, extremely long-blooming
• 'Alpenglow', to 1½ feet, carmine, tolerates poor, dry soil.

Lancaster geranium

'Johnson's Blue'

'Alpenglow'

Supporting Plants

Cranesbills tend to have floppy, sprawling stems. Support stems with metal hoop stakes or simple wooden frames.

'Pink Star'

Gypsophila

Gypsophila paniculata
Baby's breath

This perennial is named for its lovely clouds of little white or pink flowers. The plants' tiny flowers; multiple slender, sharply angled stems; and small leaves give them a light airy texture in the garden.

Blooming Time: Mid- to late summer; relatively short-blooming.

Hardiness: Zones 4 to 8.

Height: 1½ to 3 feet, depending on cultivar.

Spacing: 1 to 2 feet.

Light: Full sun; appreciates partial afternoon shade in warm climates.

Soil: Fertile, well-drained, neutral to slightly alkaline pH.

Moisture: Average.

Garden Uses: Although it doesn't bloom for very long, baby's breath is a wonderful filler in fresh or dried bouquets, and it can perform the same function in the garden. The plants like to spread out, and they can cover holes left by poppies, spring phlox, or spring bulbs.

Comments: Baby's breath may need staking to support the stems when plants are in bloom; make a supporting structure with four canes and wrap some twine or heavy string around them.

Recommended Cultivars:
- 'Perfecta', 3–4 ft.; double white flowers
- 'Pink Fairy', 1½ ft.; pale pink flowers

Drying Baby's Breath
Baby's breath air-dries beautifully. Gather stems in bunches with rubber bands and hang upside down in an airy location until they are completely dry.

Baby's breath makes an excellent filler in fresh arrangements

Christmas rose

Helleborus

Helleborus niger, Christmas rose
Helleborus orientalis, also known as
H. x hybridus, Lenten rose

Christmas roses bear white flowers that turn pinkish as they age; the divided evergreen leaves are a deep green and have toothed edges. The later-blooming Lenten roses bear clusters of drooping bell-shaped flowers in pale greenish white or pale pink to deep maroon-pink. The leaves of both species are glossy green and divided with sharply toothed edges.

Blooming Time: Christmas roses bloom in the winter in mild climates and in early spring in areas where the soil freezes. Lenten roses bloom in early spring.

Hardiness: Christmas rose, Zones 3 to 9; lenten rose, Zones 3 to 10.

Height: Christmas rose, 8 inches to 1 foot; lenten rose, to 2 feet.

Spacing: Christmas rose, 1½ feet; lenten rose, 2 feet.

Light: Partial or light, dappled shade.

Soil: Cool, well-drained, fertile and rich in organic matter with a neutral to alkaline pH.

Moisture: Average to even.

Garden Uses: Grow these plants in woodland gardens, under deciduous shrubs, or in informal shady beds and borders.

Comments: Dig in lots of compost, well-aged manure, or leaf mold when you prepare the planting area, and top-dress liberally with one of these amendments once a year to keep the soil in good condition. Plants take a couple of years to get established in the garden. Christmas rose is fairly demanding in terms of its environmental conditions, but the rewards are worth the extra effort. It does best in light, dappled shade and in neutral to alkaline soil. Lenten rose prefers the same conditions, but is generally more adaptable to a range of soil types. It tolerates most average garden soils and is easy to grow in all but hot climates.

Once established, the plants spread very slowly, so you probably won't have to divide or move them. It's best to leave them in place because the roots do not like to be disturbed. They are likely to self-sow and form colonies. If you wish to transplant some of the volunteers, do so with great care in spring. The plants go dormant in dry summer weather and should not be disturbed at that time.

The evergreen leaves may dry out in harsh winter winds; if wind is a problem in your garden, you may wish to spray the foliage with an antitranspirant to protect it. In spring, cut off any dried out or tattered leaves to improve the overall look of the plants and make the flowers easier to see. (They can be hidden under the foliage.)

Hellebores are poisonous if ingested, and contact with the sap can cause skin irritation in sensitive individuals. Wear gloves when cutting and arranging them if you don't know if you are sensitive.

Recommended Cultivars:
• 'Atrorubens', slightly over 1 ft. tall; flowers in late winter or early spring; deep plum purple
• 'Royal Heritage', 1½–2 ft.; long-lasting when cut; purple, red, deep maroon, white, green, pink, yellow flowers

Lenten rose

Hemerocallis

Hemerocallis cultivars
Daylily

Daylilies are one of the most useful garden flowers because they are easy to grow, come in a huge range of colors, and require little care. How could a gardener go wrong with such a plant? Daylilies produce trumpet-shaped flowers on branched stems above a clump of strap-shaped leaves. Each flower lasts only one day, but plants produce many of them in succession.

Blooming Time: Summer; there are early, mid- and late season cultivars.

Hardiness: Zones 3 to 10.

Height: 1 to 5 feet.

Spacing: 1½ to 2½ feet.

Light: Full sun to partial shade; pastels hold their color better in partial shade.

Soil: Any ordinary garden soil.

Moisture: Average; can tolerate dryness but need water during prolonged drought.

Garden Uses: Plant groups in beds and borders (low growers in front, taller cultivars in the middle to back according to height) or mass along a driveway or a fence.

Comments: Plants don't need dividing very often. But after several years, they may become crowded. If you notice that the plants are producing fewer flowers than they once did, it's time to divide the tuberous roots.

'Chicago Regal'

Recommended Cultivars: There are far too many cultivars for a complete listing. A few beauties:
• 'Stella de Oro', 2 ft.; very long bloom; golden yellow
• 'Hyperion', 4 ft.; fragrant; bright lemon yellow
• 'Memorable Masterpiece', 1½ ft.; late-blooming; pale peach-pink
• 'Prairie Blue Eyes', 2 ft. or slightly taller; mid-season; lavender-blue
• *H. lilio-asphodelus* (*flava*), lemon lily; 2 ft.; fragrant; clear yellow

'Stella de Oro'

Dividing Daylilies

1. Divide daylilies in late summer after they finish blooming. Cut back leaves; dig up the clump; and pull apart the tuberous roots with your hands.
2. Check to see that all divisions have both roots and leaves; then replant immediately in the new locations. Water thoroughly.

Hibiscus

Hibiscus moscheutos
Rose mallow

Large, open cup-shaped to saucerlike flowers with prominent fused stamens in the center typify rose mallows. They bloom in shades of pink, rose, pale yellow, or white. Flowers can be 6 or more inches across; leaves are large, oval to nearly heart-shaped, on thick stems.

Blooming Time: Mid- to late summer; long-blooming.

Hardiness: Zones 5 to 10.

Height: 3 to 8 feet.

Spacing: 3 to 6 feet.

Light: Full sun.

Soil: Moist but well-drained, rich in organic matter, with neutral to mildly alkaline pH.

Moisture: Average to moist.

Garden Uses: The huge flowers and lush leaves of rose mallows bring an exotic, tropical feeling to any garden. Plant them in the back of a bed, as a border by themselves, as specimens or focal points in a lawn, or in large tubs. (Plants in tubs will remain smaller.)

Comments: The plants are not hardy north of Zone 5; gardeners in these areas grow them as annuals rather than perennials. Start plants about 6 weeks before the frost-free date or buy seedlings. Set out the plants after all danger of frost is past in spring.

There is a smaller, shrubbier-looking relative, *H. rosa-sinensis* (Chinese or Hawaiian hibiscus), with woody stems and flowers in an assortment of warm shades. This plant is widely available and is not hardy, although it looks like it should be. Unless you live in a frost-free climate, you'll have to bring this species indoors and grow it as a houseplant in winter.

'Disco Belle Red'

Recommended Cultivars:
- 'Disco Belle Pink', 2½ ft.; pink shading to white
- 'Lady Baltimore', 4 ft.; pink with red center
- 'Lord Baltimore', 4 ft.; red
- 'Blue River II', flat white flowers

'Disco Belle White'

Cutting Back Damaged Stems

In early spring, use lopping shears to cut winter-damaged stems to the ground. They will regrow from the crown of the plant and bloom as usual.

Hosta

Hosta species
Plantain lily

Hostas are grown primarily for their foliage, which comes in a range of green shades from chartreuse to blue-green. Many cultivars are variegated in gold or white, in assorted patterns. Some leaves have a puckered, quilted texture; others are smooth. The leaves are oval to elongated and grow in the form of a low rosette. Bell-shaped white or lavender flowers resembling small lilies bloom in clusters on tall stems; some are fragrant.

'Albo Picta'

Blooming time: Mid- to late summer.

Hardiness: Zones 3 to 8.

Height: Many sizes, from dwarf 6-inch cultivars to large-leaved plants with flower stems 4 or 5 feet high that rise above a 3-foot-tall mound of foliage.

Spacing: 1 to 3 feet, depending on cultivar.

Light: Partial shade to shade; some can tolerate full sun if the soil is rich and moist.

Soil: Fertile, well-drained, rich in organic matter, with a slightly acid to neutral pH.

Moisture: Even moisture in summer, drier conditions in winter when dormant.

Garden Uses: Hostas are welcome in shady gardens, where, as dictated by their size, they are effective massed in the front or middle of beds or borders. They make excellent ground covers because they add needed texture while blocking weeds.

'Gold Standard'

Comments: Hostas are easy to grow, very hardy, and seldom need division. Deadhead to keep plants looking attractive after bloom.

Recommended Cultivars: New cultivars are continually being developed, with variations in size, leaf color, texture, and variegation patterns.
- 'Abby', 8 in.; blue-green with gold-green edging
- 'Bright Lights', 1¼ ft.; grows well in Zone 9; puckered golden leaves with blue- green edging
- 'Francee', to 2 ft.; deep green with white edges
- 'Gold Standard', to 1¼ ft.; yellow-green leaves with darker green edging
- 'Krossa Regal', 2 ft.; blue-green leaves
- 'Royal Standard', 2 ft.; light green leaves, white flowers
- 'Sum and Substance', 2½ ft.; yellow-green; deep veins
- *H. sieboldiana* 'Elegans', 2½ ft.; wide blue-green leaves
- 'Frances Williams', 2½ ft.; quilted blue-green leaves irregularly edged in gold

Saving Sunflower Seeds

1. It's time to divide hosta plants when the central stems die out and the clumps appear empty in the center.
2. After blooming is finished, dig the clump out of the ground. Use the shovel as a lever to raise the root ball.

3. Pull or cut apart the clump, discarding the old central portion and retaining the younger outer parts.
4. Cut back the stems to leave only a few inches, and replant the divisions immediately. Water the plants well.

Iberis

Iberis sempervirens
Perennial Candytuft

Candytufts are versatile, easy-to-grow plants with a variety of uses in the garden. They form a low spreading mat of narrow dark green leaves that are evergreen in mild climates. In spring they bear dainty, rounded clusters of tiny pure white flowers.

Blooming Time: Mid-spring.

Hardiness: Zones 3 to 8.

Height: 8 to 10 inches.

Spacing: 1 foot.

Light: Full sun.

Soil: Rich, well-drained.

Moisture: Even moisture produces the best bloom; water during dry spells.

Garden Uses: Use candytuft in the front of beds or borders, in rock gardens, along sidewalks or paths, next to driveways, or spilling over retaining walls. Candytuft makes a good companion for tulips and other later spring bulbs.

Comments: Shearing back plants after the first flush of flowers fades prompts them to bloom again. In cold climates, trim off dead leaf tips at the end of winter to encourage new green growth. Propagate new plants by division or from leaf cuttings taken in late summer. Annual forms of candytuft are also available. While some are only 4 or 5 inches tall, others are up to 8 inches. Unlike perennial candytuft, they are available in shades of rose as well as pure white.

Annual candytuft (I. umbellata)

'Improved White Spiral'

Recommended Cultivars:
• 'Snowflake', to 10 in.; larger flower heads than the species form
• 'Snow White', 6 in.; long-lived
• 'Purity', long blooming
• 'Nana', to 6 in.; more upright, rather than spreading, habit
• 'Autumn Beauty', flowers in spring and reliably in autumn if sheared back after the first bloom

Combining Plants

Low-growing candytuft makes a good understory plant for shrubs such as this camellia. The combination is particulary effective if the plants bloom at the same time.

Iris

Iris species
Iris

Stately, elegant irises have been favorites among both gardeners and artists for centuries. Most irises grow from rhizomes (some grow from bulbs), but all are distinguished by their straight, tall, swordlike or grassy leaves. Iris flowers consist of narrow, inner, petal-like structures called *style branches*, three upright petals called *standards*, and three drooping outer sepals called *falls*.

Irises are named for the Greek goddess of the rainbow, and they come in a rainbow of colors. The range includes white, ivory, many yellow shades, gold, apricot, orange, pinks, magenta, maroon, brownish red, lavender, blues, purples, violets, and deep purple-black. Many have falls of one color and standards of another; the style branches on others differ in color from the falls and standards.

Irises are divided into a number of classes. Among gardeners the best known types are bearded (tall, intermediate, dwarf), spuria, Siberian, Louisiana, and Japanese irises.

Blooming Time: Late spring. Individual cultivars have a short blooming period—one to three weeks—so plant several types to extend the season. With careful planning, you can have irises blooming until high summer.

Bulbous irises are the earliest to bloom. (See "Introducing Bulbs," page 70.) Next come the dwarf types, followed by the intermediates (which flower along with tulips). They are succeeded by the tall bearded cultivars.

Dwarf iris

Japanese iris

Removing Rhizome Rot

1. Suspect rhizome rot if leaves begin to yellow and turn brown. Pull back the leaves and carefully examine the rhizome.

2. Use a spoon to scoop out all the soft, rotted portions of the rhizome, cutting just beyond the rot.

3. Pour ordinary laundry bleach on the remaining rhizome. It kills the disease organisms without hurting the plant.

Next come the spurias, then Siberians, and finally, the Japanese and Louisiana types.

Hardiness: Varies with type and cultivar; most don't grow well in the extreme North or South.

Height: 4 inches to 5 feet.

Spacing: 8 inches to 2½ feet, varies with type.

Light: Full sun; some afternoon shade in warm climates.

Soil: Well-drained, humusy, fertile.

Moisture: Average to abundant, varies with type.

Garden Uses: There are irises for the back of beds and borders, rock gardens, bog and water gardens, cutting gardens, and naturalistic gardens. Plant irises in their own beds, in combination with other perennials or annuals, along walks and driveways, in front of a hedge or wall, or in clumps in mixed flower gardens.

Comments: When planting bearded irises, dig a deep hole and make a mound in the center of it. The top of the mound should be level with the surrounding soil. Set the rhizome horizontally on the mound and spread the roots down over it. Fill the hole with soil; firm it around the roots; and water thoroughly. Don't cover the rhizomes with soil (except in hot climates). Plant with the fan of leaves pointing in the direction you want the plants to grow.

Plant new irises, or dig and divide crowded clumps after their blooming season ends in your area. In warmer zones, wait until fall. When dividing, discard the woody inner portion of the root clump and replant the outer portions. Divide bearded iris every three or four years and Siberians whenever clumps become crowded.

Bearded iris

Recommended Cultivars: There are far too many excellent iris cultivars to attempt a reasonable listing. Choose cultivars of all types according to your preferences for size and color as well as the plants' blooming season.

Dividing Irises

1. Every few years, divide bearded irises in midsummer when they finish blooming. Dig the rhizomes from the ground, taking the roots, too.
2. Examine the rhizomes carefully and cut them into pieces, each of which with at least one fan of leaves. Discard old, woody pieces of rhizome.
3. Cut back the stems. If your plants have had any fungal diseases, dust the rhizomes with powdered sulfur or another fungicide before replanting.
4. Replant the divisions immediately, setting the rhizomes so their tops are partially exposed or only very thinly covered with soil.

Siberian iris

Lavandula

Lavandula angustifolia
English lavender

Lavender flowers range in color from lavender to deep violet. Small spikes of the tiny flowers grow at the top of slender, wandlike stems. The shrubby, sprawling plants have silvery green leaves and stems that become woody with age. Both flowers and leaves possess a distinctive, refreshing fragrance. There is also a white-flowered form.

Blooming Time: Midsummer.

Hardiness: Zones 5 to 8.

Height: 1 to 3 feet, depending on cultivar.

Spacing: 1½ to 3 feet, depending on the cultivar and growing conditions.

Light: Full sun.

Soil: Light, well-drained, gravelly soil is ideal. Lavender needs a near-neutral pH and does not thrive in dense, soggy soil.

Moisture: Average to occasionally dry.

Garden Uses: Loved for its fresh, clean scent, lavender is as at much at home in the front of a flower garden as it is in an herb garden. It is heavenly planted in masses or

'Hidcote Blue'

along the edge of a path where passersby will brush against it and release the scent.

Comments: Lavender tolerates heat and drought. In the southeastern U.S., especially in Zones 9 to 11, it is best-grown as an annual because it doesn't fare well in very humid conditions. In cold, windy locations, mulch plants well for winter protection. 'Munstead' often survives in Zone 4 with a deep winter mulch.

Recommended Cultivars:
• 'Hidcote', 1 ft. or slightly taller, deep violet
• 'Munstead', to 1½ ft.; purple, very fragrant
• 'Munstead Dwarf', 1 ft.; deep purple
• 'Rosea', slightly over 1 ft., pink
• 'Lavender Lady', 8–10 in.; traditional lavender; blooms first year from seed but not reliably hardy in cold climates.

'Munstead Dwarf'

Cutting Back Lavender Stems

Cut back lavender plants in early spring each year to give them a tidy, symmetrical form.

Liatris

Liatris spicata
Blazing star, Spike gayfeather

Blazing stars' straight vertical stems are topped in summer with vertical purplish pink or white spikes that resemble bottle brushes. The tiny flowers clustered along each spike open from the top down. The stems rise above a clump of narrow, pointed leaves shaped like broad blades of grass.

Blooming Time: Midsummer into fall.

Hardiness: Zones 3 to 9.

Height: 2 to 4 feet, depending on cultivar.

Spacing: 1 to 1½ feet.

Light: Full sun.

Soil: Well-drained, humusy, average fertility; good drainage is important in winter.

Moisture: Average to even.

Garden Uses: A good plant for providing a vertical line or a spiky form in a bed or border, blazing star is also nice in meadow and prairie gardens. The flowers are good for cutting and drying. They attract butterflies, too.

Comments: Blazing stars are easy to grow. Divide plants in early spring if bloom decreases after several years.

Recommended Cultivars:
• 'Kobold', 2–2½ ft.; reddish purple
• 'Snow Queen', 2½ ft.; white

'Alba'

'Kobold'

Cutting Liatris for the Vase

Liatris is an excellent cut flower. Cut stems when about half the flowers on the spike have opened, as shown in the inset below. The white flowers are past their prime and should not be cut.

Cut a vertical slit in the bottom of each stem and condition in a container of water nearly up to the base of the flower for several hours before arranging.

Saving Liatris Seeds

Save seed from liatris at the end of the season. Wait until the seed spike has dried but cut them before the seeds shatter.

'Desdemona'

Ligularia

Ligularia species
Ligularia

These big, imposing plants have presence in shady gardens. They form mounds of large, triangular or kidney-shaped toothed leaves and bright yellow or orange flowers. Flowers of L. dentata are daisylike and carried in clusters; those of *L. stenocephala* appear in an upright spike.

Blooming Time: Early to late summer, depending on cultivar.

Hardiness: Zones 4 to 8; grows best where summers are cool.

Height: 3 to 6 feet, varies with cultivar.

Spacing: 2 to 3 feet.

Light: Full sun to light shade; needs afternoon shade in warmer climates.

Soil: Well-drained, fertile and humusy.

Moisture: Even to abundant.

Garden Uses: Use ligularia in the back of beds and borders or in moist, shady spots where you can give it plenty of room. It is lovely when used around a water garden or

'The Rocket'

in a garden at the edge of a woodland. It self-seeds easily and is an excellent choice for a plant to naturalize in moist, partially shaded areas.

Comments: Slugs may be a problem. Trap them as shown below or set out boards next to the plants in the evening. Slugs will crawl under these boards once the sun rises and you'll be able to catch and dispose of them in the morning. Use kitchen tongs to pick them up if you don't want to touch them.

Water ligularia during spells of dry weather. In cold zones, mulch during the winter.

Recommended cultivars:
- *L. dentata* 'Desdemona', to 3 ft.; purple stems and leaf undersides, orange flowers
- 'Othello', to 3 ft.; similar coloration to 'Desdemona' but blooms later
- *L. stenocephala* 'The Rocket', 5–6 ft.; yellow flowers

SMART TIP

Controlling Slugs
Stale beer is a good slug trap. Set beer-filled cans flush with the soil surface if possible. However, slugs are so attracted to beer that they may crawl up a can to find it.

Lobelia

Lobelia cardinalis
Cardinal flower
Lobelia siphilitica
Great blue lobelia

These lobelia species are both wildflowers native to eastern North America. Cardinal flower bears spikes of brilliant scarlet fringed flowers above a low clump of deep green, lance-shaped leaves. Great blue lobelia has spikes of small blue to violet blossoms similar in form to those of cardinal flower; it, too, has lance-shaped leaves.

Blooming Time: Cardinal flower, late summer; great blue lobelia, late summer into fall.

Hardiness: Cardinal flower, Zones 2 to 9; great blue lobelia, Zones 4 to 9.

Height: Cardinal flower, 2 to 4 feet; great blue lobelia, 2 to 3 feet.

Spacing: 1 foot.

Light: Full sun to light or partial shade.

Soil: Average to fertile, humusy.

Moisture: Even to moist or even periodically wet.

Garden Uses: Both species are lovely in moist meadow gardens, wildflower gardens, and alongside a stream or pond. Cardinal flower attracts hummingbirds.

Comments: Plants tend to be short-lived in gardens and may need to be replaced every few years. Great blue lobelia usually takes to domestication better than cardinal flower. Give both species a winter mulch.

Recommended Cultivars:
L. cardinalis:
• 'Alba' and 'Gladys Lindley', white flowers
• 'Rose Beacon' and 'Twilight Zone', pink flowers
• 'Compliment Scarlet', with large scarlet flowers
L. siphilitica:
• 'Alba', white flowers
• 'Nana', a dwarf cultivar with blue flowers
• 'Blue Peter', especially nice blue flowers.

Cardinal flower

Great blue lobelia

SMART TIP

Managing Lobelia Volunteers
Lobelia species self-seed easily. Thin or transplant the volunteers to new garden spots when they have their first true leaves.

Monarda

Monarda didyma
Bee balm

Bee balms produce clusters of tubular flowers surrounded by slender bracts (modified leaves), in shades of red, pink, purple, and white, at the top of their numerous tall, straight stems. Pairs of aromatic, oval, dark green leaves line the square stems.

'Cambridge Scarlet'

'Petite Delight'

Blooming Time: Summer.

Hardiness: Zones 4 to 9.

Height: 2½ to 3 feet.

Spacing: 1½ feet.

Light: Full sun to partial shade.

Soil: Fertile, rich in organic matter.

Moisture: Even; does not do well in dry soil.

Garden Uses: Bee balm is noteworthy for its unusual flower clusters and fragrant leaves. An attractive plant for the middle or back of the garden, it works best in informal designs. Bee balm flowers attract bees and scarlet-flowered types also attract hummingbirds.

The leaves can be dried and used for tea. The flavor is citrusy, containing notes of both orange and lemon. Bee balm leaves give Earl Grey tea its distinctive flavor. You can also add chopped fresh leaves and flowers to green salads or fruit salads, or use the flowers as a colorful edible garnish on salads or dishes where the citrus note will complement the flavors. To use bee balm as a cut flower, cut stems when the first few flowers in the cluster have opened. Strip off the lower leaves, then stand the stems in cool water nearly to the base of the flowers for a few hours before arranging.

Bee balm flowers can be dried to use in wreaths and arrangements. Although red ones lose some of their brightness during drying, they still add color to craft projects. Dried leaves and flowers are lovely in potpourris. Hang bunches of flowers upside down in a dark, dry airy place to air-dry them.

Comments: A member of the mint family, bee balm spreads like its relatives and can become invasive. Avoid problems by growing plants in pots that you sink in the garden. Powdery mildew can attack leaves in late summer. Plantings will need division every two or three years.

Recommended Cultivars:
All are milldew resistant.
- 'Gardenview Scarlet', to 3 ft.; bright scarlet flowers
- 'Marshall's Delight', to 3½ ft.; pink flowers
- 'Petite Delight', slightly over 1 ft. tall, rose pink flowers,

Cutting Back Bee Balm

Bee balm is prone to various fungus diseases. If plants begin to look ratty in the late summer, cut back the stems and remove them from the garden. The new growth will be more vigorous.

Milky bellflower

Carpathian harebell, 'Alba'

Clustered bellflower

Oenothera

Oenothera speciosa
Showy primrose
Oenothera fruticosa
Sundrops

These are two day-blooming members of the evening primrose clan. Showy primrose bears cup-shaped light pink flowers above bushy mounds of narrow gray-green leaves. The petals are marked with darker pink along the veins and at the margins and have bright yellow stamens that arise from a yellow throat. Sundrops produce the same sort of cup-shaped blossoms, but these are a cheery bright yellow color. They are also slightly taller and more bushlike, with many branched stems. The oval leaves are a deep green color and have smooth margins.

Blooming Time: Both flower through much of the summer months.

Hardiness: Zones 4 or 5 to 9.

Height: 1 to 2 feet.

Spacing: 1½ to 2 feet.

Light: Full sun.

Soil: Well-drained, average to poor fertility.

Moisture: Average; tolerates drought.

Garden Uses: Nice additions to informal beds and borders.

Comments: Flowers of both species can coat the foliage when in full bloom, so a mass planting can make a very showy display. However, if they are grown in rich soil, the plants produce lush foliage but fewer flowers.

Both species are easy to start from seed. Plant them indoors about 8 weeks before the frost-free date and transplant to the garden after all danger of frost has passed.

Divide crowded plants in spring. Showy primrose can be invasive.

Recommended Cultivars:
• *O. speciosa* 'Rosea', 1¼ ft.; clear pink flowers
• *O. fruticosa* 'Sonnenwende' ('Summer Solstice'), long-blooming with burgundy-red leaves in autumn

SMART TIP

Planting Oenothera Seeds
Sow seeds as usual in a flat or cell tray. They require darkness to germinate; cover the flat with plastic film to retain moisture, and then newspaper to exclude light.

Paeonia

Paeonia species
Peony

Peonies are among the most beloved garden flowers. Their huge single or double blossoms are showy, and sweetly fragrant in some cultivars. The plants are easy to grow, dependable bloomers that live long and ask little of the gardener. The flowers come in many shades of red, rose, and pink, as well as cream and white. Peonies die back to the ground in winter, but during the growing season they are large bushy plants with attractive lobed and divided leaves.

There are a number of flower forms. Single-flowered types have five or more petals with colorful stamens in the center. Japanese peonies, also known as anemone forms, are similar. They have one or two rows of petals and a larger pom-pom-like tuft of stamens in the center. Double-flowered peonies are the most familiar, with big, full blossoms.

Blooming Time: Late spring to early summer.

Hardiness: Zones 2 to 8.

Height: 1½ to 3½ feet.

Spacing: 2 to 3 feet.

Light: Full sun is best; tolerates partial shade.

Soil: Well-drained, humusy, slightly acidic.

Moisture: Average.

Garden Uses: With foliage that maintains its good looks all season, as well as its graceful form and lovely blooms, peonies are wonderful plants for beds and borders. On their own, they also make a handsome border or divider in the yard, and they are delightful lining a driveway or path. Or use them as specimens or focal points in a lawn. They make marvellous cut flowers.

Cut peonies when the buds are showing color but before the flowers open. Cut the flowers in the morning or early evening. Split the ends of the thick stems in cool water containing a little sugar or some commercial cut flower preservative. Let the flowers stand in the water for several hours to condition them. Recut the stems when you arrange the flowers. Cut peonies are magnificent in a bowl by themselves or in a mixed arrangement with smaller flowers in a variety of shapes.

'Sarah Bernhardt'

SMART TIP

Siting Peonies
Peonies become large bushes in only a few short months each year. Their dark green, lobed leaves and graceful, vase-shaped form make them attractive additions to the landscape, whether they are in bloom or not. Plant them in a location where you want a seasonal focal point.

Comments: Strong winds can damage peony flowers, so plant them in a sheltered location if you can. Don't plant them too shallow or too deep, or they may not bloom—set the crowns 1 to 2 inches below the soil surface. Peonies seldom need dividing. Feed them once a year, in spring, with a balanced all-purpose fertilizer. In cold climate gardens, mulch them for the winter. Plants sometimes need staking to keep them upright.

When you cut peonies for the vase, take buds that are just beginning to open. If you notice ants crawling on the buds, don't be alarmed. They are there to eat a sweet syrup covering the buds. Shake them off any flowers you cut to bring indoors.

Recommended Cultivars: There are many fine peony cultivars on the market. Following are a few of the best:
- 'Bowl of Cream', 2½ ft.; midseason; double white flowers
- 'Coral Charm', 3 ft.; early; semidouble coral flowers
- 'Festiva Maxima', to 3 ft.; early; double white flowers
- 'Karl Rosenfield', 2½ ft.; midseason; double red flowers
- 'Monsieur Jules Elie', to 3 ft.; early; double pink flowers
- 'Sarah Bernhardt', 3 ft.; late blooming; double light pink, fragrant flowers flecked with red

'Mitama'

'Bowl of Beauty'

'Red Charm'

Papaver

Papaver nudicaule
Iceland poppy
Papaver orientale
Oriental poppy

Iceland and Oriental poppies are classic late-spring flowers that bloom in a wide range of lovely colors. Their silky, ruffled petals resemble tissue paper. Flowers bloom at the top of tall, slender stems that rise above a basal mound of hairy, divided leaves.

Blooming Time: Late spring.

Hardiness: Iceland poppy, Zones 2 to 10; Oriental poppy, Zones 3 to 9.

Height: Iceland poppy, 1 to 2 feet; Oriental poppy, 1½ to 4 feet.

Spacing: Iceland poppy, 1½ feet; Oriental poppy, 2 to 3 feet.

Light: Full sun; partial shade in warm climates.

Soil: Light, sandy or loamy, plenty of organic matter.

Moisture: Average to moist when in active growth.

Garden Uses: Poppies are lovely in mixed beds and borders where they add color to the middle or back areas. They drop their petals when cut unless you sear their stems in flame just after cutting. The seedpods are interesting in dried arrangements.

Comments: Plant Iceland poppies in early spring in most climates and in autumn in the South and Pacific Northwest. Many gardeners prefer to grow them as annuals.

Iceland poppy

Oriental poppies are grown much like Iceland poppies, but they prefer a somewhat richer soil. Plant bare-root Oriental poppies in the fall. The tall plants may need to be staked. Don't move or divide plants for a few years after planting to allow them time to establish themselves and develop their full beauty. Thereafter, move them in the fall, but only if it's necessary. Mulch the plants in fall with an inch-deep layer of compost or well-aged manure.

Recommended Cultivars:
Iceland poppy:
• 'Sherbet' series, just over 1 ft.; pastel peach, yellow and white, or a bright mix of red, orange, rose, cream
• 'Parfum Mix', 1 ft.; red, orange, pink, yellow, bicolors
Oriental poppy:
• 'Helen Elizabeth', 2½ ft.; early; salmon flowers; ruffled
• 'Pizzicato Mix', 1½ ft.; grow from seed; red, pink, mauve, salmon, white
• 'Raspberry Queen', 2½ ft.; midseason; raspberry pink flowers with black blotches in the center
• Türkenlouis', 3–3½ ft.; red flowers with fringed petals
• 'White King', 3–3½ ft.; early; white flowers with purple-black central blotches

Cutting Back for Regrowth

1. Divide crowded oriental poppies in late summer when they produce a new rosette of leaves. Pull clumps apart gently.

2. Replant the divisions immediately in moist, humusy soil. Plant them at the same depth they were growing.

3. Firm the soil around the new plants; water; and mulch with a loose organic material to conserve soil moisture.

Beard-tongue (P. calcycosus)

Penstemon

Penstemon species
Beard-tongue

Beard-tongues bloom in shades of pink, blue, violet, red, and sometimes white. There are 250 species and many named cultivars. The tubular, lipped flowers are clustered along slender stems that rise above a low clump of narrow leaves. Though the flowers are delightful, plants tend to be somewhat short lived and may need to be replaced after several years.

Blooming Time: Early summer to early autumn, depending on species and cultivar.

Hardiness: Zones 3 to 8.

Height: 1 to 3 feet.

Spacing: 1 to 1½ feet.

Light: Full sun.

Soil: Very well-drained, sandy or gravelly.

Moisture: Average to low; tolerates drought but not moist soils.

Garden Uses: Grow this in a rock garden or a drought-tolerant bed or border.

Comments: Good drainage is critical for beard-tongues, which are native to the American West from the Rockies to Mexico. They hold up well in hot conditions. Provide a winter mulch in colder zones. Named cultivars tolerate

ordinary garden soil somewhat better than the species. In heavy clay soils, plants are susceptible to crown rot.

Recommended Cultivars:
- 'Rose Elf', 1½–2 ft.; rose pink flowers
- 'Elfin Pink', 1 ft.; clear pink flowers
- 'Firebird', 2½ ft.; Zones 6 to 9; bright red flowers
- 'Garnet', 2 ft.; Zones 6 to 9; garnet red flowers
- *P. digitalis* 'Husker Red', 3 ft.; white flowers; red foliage

Close-up of P. australis flower   **P. barbatus 'Coccineus'**

Saving Beard-tongue Seeds

To save seed, let some flowers mature and produce seedpods. When the seedpods are dry and dark-colored, cut them off; remove the seeds; and store the seeds in an air-tight container.

Perovskia

Perovskia atriplicifolia
Russian sage

This lovely plant has a clump of semiwoody, branched, upright stems that give the effect of a delicate, fine-textured shrub. The stems are lined with gray-green aromatic leaves that are finely cut and divided into narrow, oblong leaflets. The plants are graced with light, airy sprays of tiny tubular purple-blue flowers on silvery stems; in bloom, it looks like a lavender cloud in the garden. The square stems identify Russian sage as a member of the mint family.

Blooming Time: Mid- to late summer.

Hardiness: Zones 5 to 9.

Height: 3 to 5 feet.

Spacing: 2 feet.

Light: Full sun.

Soil: Well-drained, sandy, average fertility.

Moisture: Average; tolerates drought.

Garden Uses: Plant Russian sage for a soft, misty look in an informal summer bed or border. One interesting way to use it is to plant it in the front of the garden as a scrim through which to view other, bolder flowers behind it. Otherwise, use Russian sage in the middle ground of a large border or in the back of a garden of smaller plants. It is a good choice for a seashore garden, especially if you stake the stems to brace them against the frequent winds.

Russian sage is lovely with pink garden phlox (and lavender and white phlox cultivars as well), cosmos, sparkling white shasta daisies, deep blue salvias, golden achillea or rudbeckia, and later on, sedums and chrysanthemums. Ornamental grasses are also excellent companions for perovskia.

Comments: Easy to grow in a well-drained location; holds up well in hot weather. The plants can tolerate dry,

Russian Sage

alkaline soils. Stake the tall stems if they lean. Propagate from stem cuttings taken in summer. Cut back the stems to about a foot from the ground for winter and mulch well. Russian sage is seldom bothered by pests or diseases.

Recommended Cultivars:
• 'Blue Spire', deep blue, finely divided feathery leaves
• 'Blue Haze', leaves are not as finely cut and divided as the species; lighter blue flowers than species
• 'Filigran', 3–4 ft.; hardy to Zone 4 or even 3; feathery foliage more finely divided than that of other varieties
• *P.* x *superba* (or P.'Hybrida'), improved hybrid; more compact than the species, topping out at about 3 ft. in height; darker violet-blue flowers in clusters up to 16 in. long

Planting Nursery-Grown Russian Sage Plants

1. Plant container-grown perovskia from a local nursery in spring. Dig the hole, then slide the plant out of its pot.
2. Add or subtract soil from the hole so the plant sits at the same depth as in the pot; then firm the soil, and water well.

SMART TIP

Cutting Back Perovskia
Cut back stems in late fall; then mulch when the ground freezes.

'Starfire'

Phlox

Phlox paniculata
Garden Phlox

The tall-growing garden phlox is a mainstay of many summer perennial gardens. It blooms lavishly and for a long time, and many cultivars are available in shades of pink, purple, and white. Flowers bloom in conical clusters on top of tall stems lined with lance-shaped leaves.

Blooming Time: Summer to early fall.

Hardiness: Zones 4 to 9.

Height: 2 to 4 feet.

Spacing: 1½ to 3 feet.

Light: Full sun.

Soil: Rich, loamy, with lots of organic matter; well-drained.

Moisture: Even, abundant.

Garden Uses: Garden phlox is a mainstay of summer beds and borders, both formal and informal. Use taller cultivars in the back of the garden and shorter ones in the middle. The flowers are also excellent for cutting, and have the added benefit of a wonderfully sweet fragrance.

Comments: The plants are very hardy, but they are prone to attack by leaf spot and powdery mildew in hot, humid weather. To help prevent this, space plants far enough apart to allow air to circulate between them, and water the plants at ground level rather than sprinkling leaves from overhead. Thinning the plants, by allowing just three or four shoots to remain on each plant, promotes good air circulation, strong growth, and large, abundant flowers.

Cut the stems for arrangements when half the flowers

'Eva Cullum'

in the cluster have opened. The best time to cut is early in the morning or evening. Before you arrange the flowers, condition them by standing the stems in a container of cool water nearly up to the base of the flower heads for several hours.

Lift and divide perennial phlox about every three years, when the plants finish blooming, to maintain the vigor of the plants. Cut off the flower clusters as the blossoms fade to keep the plants blooming longer. The plants are heavy feeders and appreciate an annual topdressing of compost or well-aged manure. Scratch some all-purpose fertilizer into the soil around the plants when they start growing in spring.

Recommended Cultivars:
• 'David', 3½ ft.; long blooming, mildew resistant; white
• 'Eva Cullum', 2½ ft.; long blooming; pink with red eye
• 'The King', 2–2½ ft.; long blooming; deep purple
• 'Norah Leigh', 3 ft.; variegated leaves edged in cream, pale pink flowers with dark eye
• 'Starfire', 2–3 ft.; cherry red flowers

Preventing Self-Sowing

Prevent phlox from self-sowing by cutting off the seed stalks while seedpods are still green. To save seeds, wait to cut until the pods are brown and the seeds are mature.

Physostegia

Physostegia virginiana
Obedient plant, false dragonhead

Obedient plants get their name because you can train the flower spikes to grow in a certain direction simply by moving them into that position; they obediently remain where you put them. The tiny, tubular, two-lipped light purple or white flowers grow in spires that form in a semi-circular pattern around the stem. The plants are clump-forming with stiff upright stems clad in pairs of toothed, lance-shaped leaves. Physostegia is native to eastern North America.

Blooming Time: Summer into fall.

Hardiness: Zones 3 to 10.

Height: To 3 feet.

Spacing: 1 to 1½ feet.

Light: Full sun to partial shade.

Soil: Average fertility.

Moisture: Average to moist.

Garden Uses: Grow in beds and borders or in a cutting garden. Cut stems when the lowest flowers have opened, ideally in the morning or evening. Upper flowers will open in the vase. Place stems in a container of water nearly up to the base of the flowers for several hours for conditioning before you arrange the flowers.

'Summer Snow'

Comments: Plants spread quickly in moist, rich soil and may need dividing every two or three years. Divide in early spring before the new growth begins. Physostegia is easy to grow and well worth the space it takes.

Recommended Cultivars:
- 'Alba' and 'Summer Snow', white flowers
- 'Variegata' (subspecies *speciosa* 'Variegata'), green leaves edged in cream; pink flowers
- 'Vivid', bright rosy pink flowers
- 'Bouquet Rose', light lilac-pink flowers
- 'Galadriel', dwarf to 1½ ft.; pale pink-lavender flowers
- 'Rosea', pink flowers

Dividing Root-bound Container Plants

1. If you buy a root-bound container plant, divide it when you transplant. Cut the entire plant and root ball into sections.
2. Transplant the divided sections as usual, setting the plant at the same depth it was growing in the pot. Firm the soil, and water immediately.

Flower as seen from the back

Platycodon

Platycodon grandiflorus
Balloon flower

The interesting buds of balloon flowers really do resemble miniature balloons; they open into star-shaped flowers of blue-violet, pink, or white. The erect plants have a clump of straight stems and fairly small, toothed, oval leaves.

Blooming Time: Early to late summer.

Hardiness: Zones 4 to 8.

Height: 1½ to 2 feet.

Spacing: 1 to 1½ feet.

Light: Full sun to partial shade.

Soil: Light, well-drained, moderately fertile.

Moisture: Average to abundant.

Garden Uses: Plant balloon flower in the front or middle of the garden. It is easy to grow and has a long blooming period. The flowers, especially of taller cultivars, are good for cutting, and are lovely with shasta daisies, cosmos, achillea, rudbeckia, spiky salvia, veronica, pink phlox, physostegia, and small fillers like gypsophila and armeria.

Comments: Balloon flower is reliable, hardy, and easy to grow but does not do well in hot, humid climates. It is late to appear in the spring; don't assume you've lost it until a week or two after the soil has truly warmed.
Cut stems for arrangements when several of the flowers have opened. Early in the morning or evening when they are cool is the best time to cut. The stems bleed sap when cut; this sap fouls water in a vase. Prevent bleeding by dipping the cut stem ends quickly in boiling water or searing them over a candle flame. Then condition the flowers by standing the stems in a container of warm water for several hours.

An unopened flower bud

Recommended Cultivars:
- 'Alba', white
- 'Sentimental Blue', dwarf to 1 ft. or slightly higher; flowers a lighter blue than the species
- 'Albus' (forma *albus*), white flowers with blue veins
- 'Double Blue', double flowers of rich violet-blue
- 'Mother of Pearl' ('Perlemutterschale') and 'Shell Pink' both have pink flowers.

Platycodon

Primula

Primula species
Primrose

Botanists have given primroses a family all their own, and it's a large one—there are over three hundred kinds of primroses. Some are difficult to grow, but there are many delightful cultivars that take only minimal care.

Primroses produce their flowers in clusters above a basal mound of oblong leaves. Some species bear their flowers on tall stems; other species have short stems.

Blooming Time: Early to mid-spring in cool climates, winter in warm climates.

Polyanthus hybrids

Massed primroses

Hardiness: Zones 3 to 9, varies with species.

Height: 6 inches to 2½ feet, depending on species.

Spacing: 9 inches to 1 foot.

Light: Partial shade.

Soil: Fertile, well-drained, with an acid pH; rich in organic matter.

Moisture: Average to moist.

Garden Uses: Primroses are lovely planted under trees, alongside a stream or pond, and in the rock garden.

Comments: To prevent plants from becoming crowded, lift and divide them every few years as soon as they finish blooming. You can also propagate new plants from seed in early to mid-autumn or in early spring. Sow the seeds indoors or in a cold frame, and move transplants to their permanent garden location in spring, when all danger of frost is past. In the deep South and the Southwest, plants may have difficulty surviving. If so, grow them as annuals.

Recommended Species:
- *P. denticulata* (Drumstick primrose): 1 ft.; lavender, purple, white, pink, mauve, red cultivars
- Polyanthus hybrids: 6–10 in.; often grown as a winter annual in warm climates; shades of red, pink, mauve, lavender, purple, violet, many with a yellow eye
- *P. japonica* (Japanese primrose): 1–2 ft.; clusters of flowers on tall stems in shades of pink, red, white

Primula polyanthus, Gold Lace Group

Drumstick primrose

'Irish Eyes'

Rudbeckia

Rudbeckia fulgida, R. hirta
Orange Coneflower, Black-eyed Susan

Black-eyed Susans supply bright color to any landscape. Wild plants often grow along country roads and woodlands, while domestic cultivars add color to beds and borders. The petals of the daisylike flowers are a golden yellow to an orangy gold color; centers of most cultivars are dark brown to near-black, though one has a green center. The branched plants have lance-shaped to oval leaves.

Blooming Time: Midsummer to early autumn.

Hardiness: Zones 4 to 9.

Height: 2 to 3 feet.

Spacing: 1 to 2 feet.

Light: Full sun is best, but they tolerate some light shade.

Soil: Well-drained, average fertility.

Thompson and Morgan Mixed

Moisture: Average to moist; will tolerate dry soil.

Garden Uses: Black-eyed Susans are good, dependable plants for a meadow garden or the middle ground of an informal cutting garden.

Comments: Easy to grow and durable, the plants tolerate hot weather and some cold, as well. Rudbeckia fulgida will spread, especially in light, moist soil, and needs division about every three or four years.

Recommended Cultivars:
• 'Goldsturm', 1½–2 ft.; one of the longest bloom seasons of any perennial; many flowers
• *R. hirta* 'Gloriosa Daisy', to 2 ft.; yellow petals flushed with varying amounts of mahogany red around the center

SMART TIP

Saving Rudbeckia Seeds
Let some flowers mature on the plants; then cut off the seed heads when they're brown and dry.

Cutting Rudbeckias for the Vase

When using rudbeckias as cut flowers, remove all leaves that would be underwater in the vase before you arrange the flowers, or they will foul the water.

Massed salvias

Salvia

S. x superba
Salvia, Violet sage, Ornamental sage

This hybrid was created by crossing several salvia species. It's sold under various names, so shop for particular cultivars, including those suggested below. The best-known perennial salvias bear slender upright spikes of tiny violet or purple flowers and have oblong grayish green leaves.

Blooming Time: Late spring to summer.

'Blue Hill'

Hardiness: Zones 5 to 10.

Height: 1½ to 3 feet.

Spacing: 1½ to 2 feet.

Light: Full sun.

Soil: Light, well-drained; thrives in any good garden soil.

Moisture: Average; tolerates some dryness, but needs to be watered during extended dry spells.

Garden Uses: The flowers are a welcome addition to summer flower gardens and cut flower arrangements. They are beautiful paired with soft yellows, such as *Achillea* 'Moonshine' or *Coreopsis* 'Moonbeam'.

Comments: New plants are easily propagated from cuttings, divisions, or seeds. Start seeds indoors, six to ten weeks before the last expected frost. Take cuttings in early fall or early spring. Dig and divide crowded plants in early fall or early to mid-spring.

Mexican Bush sage, *Salvia leucantha*, is also useful in the home landscape. It can help to anchor a bed or border and is a lovely sight in bloom.

Salvia is a good cut flower for fresh arrangments and can also be dried. The slender flower spikes add a welcome vertical line to arrangements of round, daisylike, and cup-shaped flowers. Cut stems when the lower flowers on the spike have opened. Place the stems in a container of warm water for several hours to condition them before arranging. The flowers last about a week.

To dry salvia flowers, hang bunches of stems upside down to air-dry, or lay stems horizontally in silica gel.

Recommended Cultivars:
- 'Blue Hill', true blue flowers
- 'East Friesland', rich blue-violet flowers
- 'May Night', deep violet-blue flowers

SMART TIP

Thinning Salvia Volunteers
Salvia species self-seed easily. Use small scissors to thin the volunteer seedlings when they appear in early spring.

Scabiosa

Scabiosa caucasica
Pincushion flower

These plants get their nickname from the structure of their domed lavender-blue or pink flower heads. The blooms consist of outer rings of small-petaled flowers surroundng a rounded center of tiny tubular flowers with prominent stamens that resemble pinheads.

Blooming Time: Mid- to late summer.

Hardiness: Zones 3 to 8.

Height: 1½ to 2½ feet.

Spacing: 1 to 2 feet.

Light: Full sun.

Soil: Well-drained, humusy, neutral to slightly alkaline pH.

Moisture: Average to even.

Garden Uses: Scabiosas are a delightful addition to a cottage garden, perennial garden, mixed bed or border, or a cutting garden. Though not long blooming, they add a light, airy texture to the middle ground of a bed or border.

Comments: Pincushion flowers like moisture but do not tolerate wet, soggy conditions. Divide mature plants in spring every four years. Blooms of pincushion flower are excellent cut flowers. The unusual structure of the flowers, along with the softness of their colors, adds sophistication to any arrangement. Cut the flowers when at least half of the florets in the flower head have opened. Cut in the early morning or evening if possible; pincushion flowers last up to a week. Strip off all foliage that would be below the water level in the vase; cut vertical slits into the bottom of each stem; keep the stems in cold water for several hours before arranging.

Recommended Cultivars:
S. caucasica:
• 'Alba', white flowers
• 'Miss Willmott', white flowers
• 'Fama', rich blue flowers to 3 in. across, on 2-ft. stems
S. columbaria:
• 'Butterfly Blue', dwarf hybrid to 15 in. tall; blooms from spring well into fall; violet-blue blossoms
• 'Pink Mist', 1–1¼ ft. tall, lilac-pink flowers

Cleaning Cell-packs

Before sowing seeds indoors, clean previously used containers and scrub them with a solution of 1 part chlorine bleach to 9 parts water. Rinse before using.

'Pink Mist'   **Pincushion flower**

SMART TIP

Deadheading Scabiosa Flowers
Deadhead pincushion flowers promptly to prolong their bloom period and keep the plants looking neat. Pinch or cut off faded flowers along with their stems.

Sedum

Sedum 'Autumn Joy'
Stonecrop

'Autumn Joy' produces tight, flattish heads of flowers that start out light green in late summer, change to pink, then rosy red, deepen to a beautiful coppery bronze that's difficult to describe, and eventually darken to a rich rust color. Light green fleshy leaves with scalloped edges grow all along the stems of these upright plants.

Blooming Time: Late summer into fall.

Hardiness: Zones 3 to 10.

Height: 1½ to 2 feet.

Spacing: 1 to 1½ feet.

Light: Full sun; tolerates light shade.

Soil: Average fertility, well-drained, especially in winter when plants are dormant.

Moisture: Plants are healthiest and produce the best blooms if they are kept on the dry side, but they will tolerate moist soil in summer as long as it is not soggy.

Planting Stonecrop in a Wall

Small sedum plants can be tucked into soil-filled niches in a stone wall or rock path. Remember to water the plants periodically.

'Autumn Joy'

Garden Uses: 'Autumn Joy' sedum is a welcome addition to an autumn garden of chrysanthemums and asters, particularly if the rusty red tones of the sedum complement the colors of the asters and chrysanthemums.

This cultivar is an outstanding garden plant—easy to grow and hard to beat for late-season color in the front to middle of the garden. The changing colors provide a long-lasting display. You can leave the flower heads on the plants all winter if you wish—they are interesting even when dry and brown.

Comments: Plants will grow in poor soil as long as it's well-drained. When plants become crowded, divide them in the spring. To propagate without dividing, take stem cuttings in early summer and transplant them into place at least a month before hard frost.

The stems and leaves of sedums contain sap that can cause skin irritation on contact and stomach discomfort if ingested. Wear gloves when cutting the blooms, taking cuttings, or even dividing.

Sedums make great cut flowers. They last more than a week in the vase, and may even form roots while in the water, like stem cuttings. Cut the flowers and place the stems in a container of water nearly up to the base of the flower heads to condition them before arranging. If the stems bleed sap when you cut them, dip the cut ends briefly into boiling water to seal them before you condition them or place them in a vase.

Sedums also dry well although the color loses its red tones and becomes more brown. Hang them upside down in small bunches to air-dry.

'Golden Fleece'

Solidago

Solidago cultivars
Goldenrod

A familiar sight in fields and along roadsides in late summer and fall, goldenrods deserve a place in the garden, too. There are numerous cultivars and hybrids with different sized and shaped flower heads, but all of them are yellow and feathery. The upright stems form clumps and have elongated leaves.

'Peter Pan'

Blooming Time: Late summer into fall.

Hardiness: Zones 5 to 9.

Height: 2 to 3½ feet.

Spacing: 1½ to 2 feet.

Light: Full sun.

Soil: Well-drained, average to low fertility.

Moisture: Average to low; tolerates drought.

Garden Uses: Goldenrod is pretty in a meadow garden, a naturalistic planting, or an informal bed or border. It makes a stunning companion to fall chrysanthemums, asters, and late-blooming annuals such as calendula.

Comments: Contrary to popular opinion, goldenrod does not cause allergies—the culprit is often ragweed, which tends to grow near goldenrod in the wild. Plants spread, and some kinds can be invasive; divide spreaders every few years to keep them in line. Hybrids have larger,

brighter colored flowers and don't spread as much as species and wild forms.

Goldenrods are lovely in autumn bouquets and arrangements, especially with asters, mums, dahlias, and monkshoods. Cut them early, when the flowers are just beginning to open. Cut stems in the morning or early evening. Condition the flowers by standing the stems in water nearly to the base of the flowers for several hours before arranging. Goldenrods also dry well. Hang them upside down in bunches to air-dry.

Recommended Cultivars:
• *S. rugosa* 'Fireworks', 3½ ft.; sprays of bright yellow flowers reminiscent of fireworks exploding in the sky
Hybrids:
• 'Golden Dwarf', 1 ft.; golden yellow flowers
• 'Peter Pan', 2 ft.; bright yellow flowers
• 'Baby Sun', 1 ft.; clear yellow flowers
• 'Golden Baby', 2 ft.; golden yellow flowers.

Goldenrod is at home in a mixed border.

Stachys

Stachys byzantina
Lamb's ears

Lamb's ears are grown primarily for their oval, softly fuzzy, green leaves covered with silver hairs. Some gardeners also enjoy the small purple flowers that they produce on tall, rather thick stems. The plants have a sprawling, spreading habit.

Blooming time: Midsummer.

Hardiness: Zones 4 to 10.

Height: Leaves grow to about 1 foot; flower stems 1½ to 2 feet.

Spacing: 1 foot.

Light: Full sun to partial shade.

Soil: Average fertility, good drainage is essential.

Moisture: Leaves will rot if the soil is too wet, but plants need water in dry weather.

Garden Uses: Lamb's ears is attractive in the front of beds and borders; if you want to let the flowers develop, plant a little farther back. The silver-white foliage beautifully complements pink, blue, and purple flowers.

'Countess Helene von Stein'

'Silver Carpet'

Comments: If leaves begin to look ratty and brown in hot summer weather, cut them back and new ones will grow. If you don't like the look of the small purple flowers, pick off the stems as they form in summer.

Recommended Cultivars:
• 'Big Ears' ('Countess Helene von Stein'), to 3 ft.; large light green leaves to 10 in. long, covered with gray-white hairs; purple flowers
• 'Silver Carpet', dwarf to 6 in. high; very silver leaves; does not bloom

Veronica

Veronica species
Speedwell

Veronicas are handsome, easy-to-grow, hardy perennials with a multiplicity of uses in flower gardens. The plants produce slender, tapered, upright spikes of little blue, purple, rose, pink, or white flowers on stems with oval to oblong leaves.

Blooming Time: Summer.

Hardiness: Zones 3 or 4 to 10, varies with species.

Height: 1 to 4 feet, varies with species.

Spacing: 1 to 1½ feet.

Light: Full sun.

Soil: Prefers reasonably fertile, well-drained soils; tolerates most average garden soils.

Moisture: Average to even.

Garden Uses: Speedwells are excellent plants for the middle of flower beds and borders.

Comments: The plants tolerate both heat and drought, but they're not always hardy in very cold winters. If you live in a very cold climate, you might want to dig up the plants in fall and put them in a cold frame over winter, just to be safe.

Most veronicas aren't grown from seed; order plants from a nursery catalog, or buy locally for spring planting. You can propagate established plants by carefully lifting and dividing them in early spring or by taking cuttings anytime during the summer growing season. Warm-climate gardeners can divide the plants in early fall after they finish blooming.

Recommended Cultivars:
• 'Goodness Grows', to slightly over 1 ft.; long blooming; deep blue
• 'Sunny Border Blue', slightly over 1 ft. to 1½ ft.; deep blue-violet flowers
• *V. peduncularis* 'Georgia Blue', 6–8 in.; grow as a ground cover; flowers are larger than most and not gathered into spikes; deep true blue flowers with a white eye
• *V. spicata* 'Red Fox', just over 1 ft.; dark rose pink flowers

Combining Speedwell in the Garden

Speedwell works well with spring bulbs, such as daffodils.

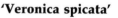
'Veronica spicata'

'Red Fox'

'Icicle'

introducing bulbs

Bulb Types Explained

A bulb is a swollen underground structure that stores nutrients. The plant draws on these supplies during its annual dormant rest period and also for leaf development. A *true bulb* is a modified flower bud and stem enclosed in thick *scales*, or enlarged overlapping leaf bases. In lilies, the scales are formed like garlic cloves; in tulips and daffodils, they grow like an onion. Bulbs' scales are anchored to a tough *basal plate*, the flat structure at the bottom of the bulb from which the roots grow.

Tulips, daffodils, and lilies are true bulbs, but the word *bulb* is often used inclusively to refer to other kinds of underground storage organs: *tubers, tuberous roots, corms,* and *rhizomes*.

A tuber (sometimes known as a *tubercorm*) is a swollen stem that usually grows underground. Roots grow from it, as do *eyes*, or buds, from which new shoots develop. Tuberous begonias, anemones, and caladiums grow from tubers.

Tuberous roots are enlarged roots that have growth buds at the crown, the area where the plant's roots meet the stems. Dahlias have tuberous roots.

A corm is the swollen base of a stem, modified to be a storage organ. Corms are usually flatter than bulbs and store their nutrients in the basal plate more than in their scales. Crocuses and gladiolus are familiar corms.

Rhizomes are underground stems that grow horizontally and produce both roots and shoots. Many plants, including some grasses and perennials, spread by means of rhizomes. Both cannas and bearded irises grow from rhizomes (though bearded iris is usually grouped with perennials rather than bulbs). Other irises, such as *I. reticulata* and Dutch hybrids, grow from bulbs.

Hardy or Tender?

Many plants categorized as bulbs are hardy to temperatures below freezing. Spring-blooming crocuses, daffodils, tulips, hyacinths, and squills are all hardy bulbs.

Other bulbs are tender, meaning that they are damaged or even killed by cold temperatures and frost. As described in "End-of-Season Activities," page 77, gardeners in cold climates lift these bulbs in autumn. Most summer-blooming bulbs, including dahlias, cannas, tuberous begonias, and gladiolus, are tender. But just because a bulb blooms in summer doesn't necessarily mean it's tender; lilies flower in summer, and many of them are very hardy. The profiles on pages 78 to 91 list the zones in which each bulb is hardy.

True Bulbs and Other Structures

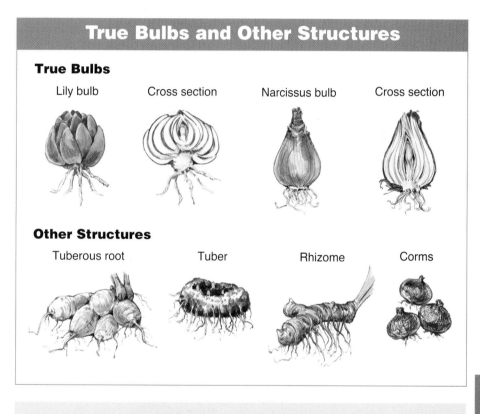

True Bulbs

Lily bulb Cross section Narcissus bulb Cross section

Other Structures

Tuberous root Tuber Rhizome Corms

Major and Minor Bulbs

Commercial bulb growers divide bulbs into two categories—major and minor. Major bulbs are the larger, flashier, more commercially important bulbs—daffodils, tulips, lilies, gladiolus, dahlias, and tuberous begonias.

The smaller and less expensive minor bulbs include grape hyacinths, squills, and species crocuses. Some catalogs now call these specialty bulbs instead of minor bulbs. By either name, minor bulbs are individually less showy than the majors, but they are still an important source of springtime color. Plant them in a mass so that their colors make an impact.

What Bulbs Do in the Garden

Early bulbs welcome spring to many gardens. From the first snowdrops and species crocuses to the elegant hybrid tulips of midspring, bulbs are unequalled as a source of early color. They bloom in many colors, sizes, and shapes, and you can mix and match them in endless combinations. Once planted, they come back year after year with only minimal maintenance.

Designing with Bulbs

The smaller, or minor, bulbs—crocuses, scillas, grape hyacinths, and snowdrops among them—are lovely massed to form carpets of color. Plant them in areas that can be left unmowed while the foliage matures—in lawns, open woodlands, under deciduous trees, or on slopes and banks. These little charmers look good in beds and borders, too, if you plant dozens or scores of them rather than clumps of threes or fives. Like undisturbed daffodils, many spread and form colonies that expand and eventually cover whole swaths of ground. This process is called naturalizing.

Using Major Bulbs. The larger bulbs—daffodils, tulips, and crown imperials, for instance—are most at home in beds and borders, especially in combination with shrubs, perennials, and annuals. One way to bring color to the garden from spring to fall is to plant annuals among and around the spring bulbs to hide their maturing foliage and carry on the show throughout the summer. Spring perennials such as candytuft and columbine also make good companions for bulbs.

Bulbs in Summer and Fall

Although many gardeners associate bulbs with spring, numerous lovely summer flowers also grow from bulbs. In zones 7 and cooler, most summer bulbs must be planted each spring, dug each fall, and stored

Bulbs are lovely naturalized in a lawn where the grass can be left unmowed in spring until the bulb foliage ripens. This lawn is graced by tulips, daffodils, anemones, and spring starflowers (*Ipheion uniflorum*).

indoors over the winter. But the result is worth the extra work.

Cut flowers. Plant gladiolus every two weeks or so for armloads of tall, spiky cut flowers throughout the summer. Hardy alliums send up their big starry globes of purple, white, or yellow from early to midsummer, and dahlias light up the garden with their huge variety of colors, sizes, and flower forms in late summer and fall.

In beds and or borders. A classic in summer beds and borders, lilies offer a wide assortment of flower sizes, colors, and blooming times. Lily flowers are more-or-less trumpet shaped; the petals vary in width, and some lilies have reflexed, (backward curving) petals. Many lilies are fragrant, and some are flushed or spotted with a second color. Best of all, many lilies are very hardy and can be left in the garden year-round.

Tuberous begonias bring bold bursts of color to shady summer gardens and container plantings. Their big blossoms may be shaped like camellias or roses, or fringed like carnations.

For a touch of the tropics, turn to cannas or caladiums. Late bloomers include colchicums, autumn crocuses, and hardy cyclamen.

Bulbs add color to summer gardens too. Here, Gladiolus 'Violetta' blooms along with catmint and 'Sparrleshoop', a climbing rose.

Planting Bulbs

In colder climates, daffodils, tulips, and other hardy spring-bloomers should be planted in early to mid-autumn, before the first hard frost. In warm climates, plant bulbs in November (or even December where winters are very mild). To stimulate blooming in warm climates, you may need to refrigerate hardy bulbs for six to eight weeks before you plant them. Ask a gardening friend or the Cooperative Extension Service if this is necessary in your area.

For the best display, plant the bulbs in drifts or in clusters of 12 or more. Plant lots more if the bulbs are small.

Preparing Bulb Sites. Hardy bulbs thrive in almost any well-drained soil, in full sun or partial shade. Ideally, you should amend their site a season before planting. But if you haven't prepared the area in advance, begin by loosening the soil and digging in an all-purpose fertilizer or a special bulb formula and plenty of organic matter. Add some gypsum and rock phosphate or superphosphate for long-term supplies of calcium and phosphorus. If your soil is sandy or contains a lot of clay, be sure to add extra leaf mold, compost, or peat moss; abundant organic matter will help improve these soils. Then rake the soil surface smooth.

If you're planting a small number of bulbs, make holes of the required depth with a trowel or a bulb planter. But to plant a lot of bulbs in the same area, it's easier to excavate it all at once with a shovel.

Placing the Bulbs. Plant the bulbs with their pointed ends up. Set one bulb in each hole or, in a larger planting, place them at the correct spacing on the bottom of the excavated area. To make the planting look more natural, gently toss them onto the area and plant them where they land.

Set the bulbs firmly in the soil at the correct depth. (See the table above.) Bury them with soil; water thoroughly; and cover the bed with a 2- to 3-inch layer of shredded leaves or other loose mulch.

Bulb Planting Depths

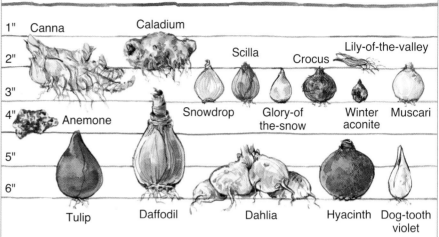

Soil Line

1" Canna — Caladium — Scilla — Crocus — Lily-of-the-valley
2"
3"
4" Anemone — Snowdrop — Glory-of-the-snow — Winter aconite — Muscari
5"
6"
Tulip — Daffodil — Dahlia — Hyacinth — Dog-tooth violet

A Rule of Thumb. If you don't know how deep to plant a bulb, use this rule of thumb: set the bulb in a hole that is 2½ times as deep as the bulb's diameter. If you're planting in heavy clay soil, don't plant quite so deep. In light, sandy soil, plant a bit deeper. But when in doubt, err on the side of deeper.

Buying and Storing Bulbs

Handle bulbs with care. Even though they're dormant when you buy them, they are still alive and are affected by their environment. If they get too wet, they'll rot; if left in hot sunlight, they'll dry out; and if sealed in a plastic bag, they'll suffocate. Such compromised bulbs won't bloom well, and may not even survive. So treat newly purchased bulbs with respect.

Shop wisely, too. If you buy bulbs locally, examine them carefully. If you order by mail, unpack the bulbs as soon as they arrive and look them over. Most healthy bulbs are firm to the touch. Anemone tubers look shriveled and dried up even when healthy, but most bulbs should be full and plump. You should feel no soft spots, nor see any evidence of rot or mold. The basal plate on the bottom of the bulb should be firm and solid, and show no mold or other damage. If the basal plate is damaged, the bulb may fail to flower or at best, will bloom poorly.

Always buy nursery-grown bulbs, never *wild-crafted* (collected from sites where they grow naturally). Wild-crafting depletes the populations of these bulbs, sometimes endangering them. Look for a "Commercially Propagated" label on bags, or ask the supplier about the bulbs' origins. Be particularly careful when buying *Anemone blanda, Cyclamen* species, *Eranthis,* and small or species *Narcissus.*

Store them in a cool, airy location away from direct sun. Store the bulbs in mesh bags, put them in paper bags with plenty of room, or spread them out on open shelves in a dark area.

Naturalizing Bulbs

Naturalizing bulbs means planting them in a lawn or ground cover and then allowing them to multiply on their own and spread out. Many of the smaller bulbs are great for naturalizing. The usual procedure is to naturalize bulbs in a lawn for a cheerful, informal effect that looks as if the bulbs had come up on their own.

Quantity matters when it comes to naturalized bulbs. It takes a minimum of a dozen or so major bulbs in every clump and 18 to 24 minor ones to show up well. Keep your costs down by looking for lower-cost packages of slightly smaller bulbs for naturalizing. With good care, they soon catch up to higher-priced bulbs.

If you're planting in an existing lawn, use a sharp pointed trowel to punch holes for the bulbs. It's a time-consuming process, but it creates the most natural look. Alternatively, you could strip the sod from the area; plant the bulbs; then either replace the sod or overseed a new lawn. Sprinkle a little rock phosphate for phosphorus and gypsum for calcium into the bottom of each planting hole or the excavated area. Scratch these amendments into the soil before setting in the bulbs. Remember that any fertilizer you put on the lawn will also affect the bulbs; a high-nitrogen lawn fertilizer could hinder the bulb's flower production. Use a more balanced formula (one with more equal numbers) for the areas where bulbs grow.

Bulbs for Naturalizing

- Autumn crocus (*Colchicum autumnale*)
- Checker lily (*Fritillaria meleagris*)
- Daffodil (*Narcissus* species and hybrids)
- Dwarf iris (*Iris reticulata*)
- Glory-of-the-snow (*Chionodoxa luciliae*)
- Grape hyacinth (*Muscari* species)
- Grecian windflower (*Anemone blanda*)
- Ornamental onion (*Allium* |species)
- Siberian squill (*Scilla siberica*)
- Snowdrop (*Galanthus nivalis*)
- Spanish bluebell (*Hyacinthoides hispanica*)
- Species crocus (*Crocus* species)
- Trout lily (*Erythronium* species)

SMART TIP

Planting Tools for Bulbs

Bulb planters are especially designed for planting bulbs. There are both long- and short-handled types, and most have the depth in inches marked on the outside. To use them, just push the tool into the soil, twist it, and pull it up with the excavated core of soil inside.

A pointed trowel can also make a perfectly good planting hole and often works better than a bulb planter in heavy soil.

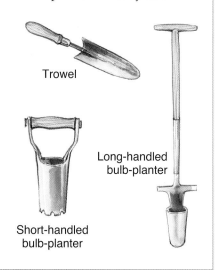

Trowel

Long-handled bulb-planter

Short-handled bulb-planter

SMART TIP

Rodent Protection

Some bulbs, such as crocuses and tulips, are candy to chipmunks and other small rodents. Keep the critters away from your bulbs by excavating entire bulb planting areas and lining the bottom and sides with hardware cloth. After planting, cover the bulbs with a sprinkling of soil and a double layer of chicken wire before adding enough soil to cover the bulbs to the correct depth. A top layer of wire offers further protection.

Species crocus naturalizes beautifully. Plant groups of crocuses in a lawn for a meadowy look in early spring.

Start tuberous begonias indoors unless you live in a warm climate with a long frost-free growing season. Plant the tubers in a flat or pots of moist potting mix, with their concave side facing upward.

Use pots of daffodils, top, for a shot of bright color. Small cultivars and species narcissus grow especially well in pots. Shown here are 'Tête-à-Tête', 'Minnow', and 'Jumblie'. Containers of `Ice Follies' daffodils, bottom, glow cheerily against evergreen shrubs.

Planting Tender Bulbs

Tender bulbs are planted like hardy bulbs, except you plant them in spring, after the danger of frost is past and the soil is warm. Prepare the soil as described under "Preparing Bulb Sites," page 73. Set the bulbs at the depth recommended in the profiles on pages 78 to 91.

If you live where the frost-free growing season is short, get a jump on the season and start some of your tender bulbs indoors. Tuberous begonias, especially, benefit from an indoor head start. Plant them in pots or flats as described below. Keep the potting mix moist but not soggy. When shoots appear, give the young plants bright light. Move them outdoors when the danger of frost is past.

Planting in Containers

Bulbs are ideal for containers. Plant pots of a single type, such as daffodils or tulips, or mix several types together.

Plant the bulbs in pots, deep flats, tubs, or planters. The containers should have drainage holes in the bottom and be at least 5 to 6 inches in diameter; flats should be 4 to 5 inches deep. Use a 5-inch bulb pan (a wide, shallow pot) to force crocuses, irises, squills, or grape hyacinths. Leave about 1½ inches between the bulbs when you plant them. They should be close together but not touching. A 6-inch pot will hold five to six tulip bulbs, three hyacinths, or three double-nosed daffodils. (A bulb's nose is the tip where stems emerge. A double-nosed bulb has two tips, usually because the bulb has propagated itself but the bulbs have not yet fully separated from each other.)

If you're reusing old pots, scrub them thoroughly and soak them in a disinfectant solution of one part liquid chlorine bleach to nine parts water before you plant. Soak clay pots in water overnight.

All bulbs need loose, crumbly soil with good drainage. A potting mix of equal parts of garden loam or potting soil, compost, peat moss, and sand is ideal. If you will discard the bulbs after they bloom, they don't need any fertilizer. They already contain the nutrients they need to produce their flowers. However, if you plan to keep the bulbs or transplant them to the garden, use a half-strength liquid fertilizer every two weeks after the shoots first appear.

In large containers outdoors, bulbs need to be planted at their regular depth. Allow ½ inch between the soil line and the rim of the pot to allow for watering.

SMART TIP

Plant a Dish Garden
It's easy to create a pretty dish garden of blooming spring bulbs. Buy several small potted bulb plants that are already in bud. Replant them in a bulb pan or a decorative ceramic dish, using a combination of large and small bulbs with flowers at different heights.

An alternative is to arrange the pots in a basket. Hide them by covering the soil and rims with long strands of sphagnum moss (the kind that hasn't been ground up). For a decorative look, tie a colorful bow on the handle of the basket.

Caring for Bulbs

Although bulbs are easy to grow, they do need some care. They appreciate a dose of fertilizer and compost once a year. To keep them blooming vigorously and increase your stock of plants, divide them after several years in the same location or whenever blooms start to diminish.

During and After Flowering

As the blossoms fade, clip them off so the bulb can channel its energy into enlarging and developing bulblets rather than producing seeds. Deadheading isn't feasible for grape hyacinths, crocuses, and other small bulbs that you grow by the dozens, but it is helpful for larger daffodils, tulips, and other major bulbs growing in beds and borders.

Most bulbs produce leaves along with their flowers, and these are an important source of nourishment for the plants. Unless you plan to dig and discard the bulbs after they bloom (as many people do with the short-lived hybrid tulips), it's essential to leave the foliage in place until it turns yellow and begins to dry out. Planting annuals or bushy perennials close to the bulb plants will help to hide the fading bulb leaves.

In the case of crocuses, grape hyacinths, and other small bulbs that you've naturalized in a lawn, wait at least six weeks after they flower before you mow the lawn where they are growing.

Fertilizing Bulbs

Small bulbs don't need to be fertilized, but larger ones benefit from feeding once or twice a year. Apply a balanced, all-purpose fertilizer as soon as the young shoots emerge from the soil, and again after the plants have finished blooming. Or you can fertilize in autumn by applying a rich compost, an all-purpose organic fertilizer blend, or a slow-release bulb fertilizer. If you don't mulch, topdress with an inch of compost or leaf mold every year to maintain a good level of organic matter in the soil.

Bulbs don't need to be watered except during prolonged dry spells when you would normally water perennials and shrubs. They seldom suffer from pest or disease problems either, as long as they are not too crowded and are grown in soils with good drainage and the appropriate pH.

Dividing Bulbs

Bulbs reproduce by means of underground offsets called bulblets that form on the outside perimeter of the bulb's basal plate. Some lilies produce bulbils—small, round structures that form in the leaf axils. Both bulblets and bulbils can be removed and planted; they eventually grow into full-size bulbs capable of producing flowers.

Corms go through an annual renewal cycle; a new corm forms on top of the old one each summer. The old corm shrivels, and the roots on the new one pull it down into the hole left by the first. Small cormlets or cormels form at the base of the new corm or, in some cases, on aboveground stems.

Tuberous roots and rhizomes are easy to divide. In the case of tuberous roots such as those of dahlias, the old tuber deteriorates as the new ones form. The new replacements can be cut into pieces, each with a bud or eye, to produce new plants. Clumps of tuberous roots can be divided like clumps of perennials.

Tubers (or tuber-corms), such as those of tuberous begonias, get larger with age. Propagate them by cutting them into large pieces, making certain that each piece has an eye or two. Let the cut surfaces callus over in the open air for a day or so before replanting.

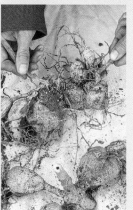

Daffodils light up a border in spring, top, when they tower above their companions. The bottom photo shows the same border in summer, when zinnias, rudbeckia, and phlox are blooming.

End-of-Season Activities

Autumn brings some special tasks to the bulb gardener. Hardy bulbs can be planted for bloom the following spring, tender bulbs can be lifted and stored safely away, and other bulbs can be prepared for forcing into winter bloom.

Lifting Tender Bulbs

When the first frost strikes, it's time to dig up tender bulbs, corms, and tubers from the outdoor garden and put them in storage for the winter. You can wait to dig most bulbs until the foliage has started to turn brown or has been softened by a light frost.

Exceptions to this rule are tuberous begonias and tuberoses, which can't tolerate even a light frost. Dig them early. If you delay digging any of the tender bulbs until you get a heavy frost, the plant crowns or the bulbs themselves may be damaged.

The basic procedure for lifting bulbs of tuberous begonias, dahlias, gladiolus, and most other tender plants with fleshy top growth is shown in the box titled "Lifting Tender Bulbs."

Mulch bulb plantings in late fall after the soil has frozen to prevent heaving damage.

Lifting Tender Bulbs

1. Wait until autumn to lift plants, such as this dahlia. Loosen the soil and lift the entire root ball as gently as possible.

2. Using a sharp pair of pruning shears, cut back the stems to several inches above the tubers.

3. With your fingers, gently remove as much soil as possible from around the tubers and roots.

4. Label the tubers as to cultivar and color, and store them in peat moss or dry leaves in a cool, dark area.

Lily leek

Allium

Allium species
Ornamental onion

The genus that gives us so many indispensable seasonings—onions, garlic, shallots, and chives—also boasts a number of ornamental species with pretty round clusters of small starry flowers. The flowers come in a range of colors (blue, purple, rose-purple, white, and yellow) and the plants in a range of sizes. All have narrow, grassy leaves and carry their blossoms at the top of straight, slender stems.

Blooming Time: Late spring to midsummer, depending on species.

Hardiness: Zones 4 to 8, varies with species.

Height: 4 inches to 4 feet, varies with species.

Persian onion

Depth and Spacing: 4 to 8 inches deep, 3 inches to 1½ feet apart, varies with species.

Light: Full sun to partial shade.

Soil: Fertile, well-drained, and sandy. (*A. neapolitanum* tolerates heavier soils.)

Moisture: Abundant, even.

Garden Uses: Ornamental onions are attractive planted in clumps in beds and borders, especially surrounded by other summer bloomers that can hide their foliage. Some make good cut flowers. Shorter-growing species are at home in a rock garden or container.

Comments: Plant alliums in fall. Divide them when the clumps become crowded and the plants begin producing fewer flowers. Tall-growers may need staking. *A. moly* and *A. neapolitanum* self-sow; deadhead to prevent unwanted seedlings.

Recommended Species:
* *A. aflatunense* Persian onion, 2–3 ft.; deep violet-purple
* *A. caeruleum* Blue-of-the-Heavens, 2 ft.; clear blue
* *A. christophii* Star of Persia, 1–2 ft.; large silvery purple globes
* *A. moly* Lily leek 'Jeannine', 1–1¼ ft.; bright yellow
* *A. neapolitanum* Daffodil garlic, to 1¼ ft.; fragrant, white
* *A. karataviense*, to 9 in.; pale pink flowers with purple midribs
* *A. sphaerocephalum* Drumstick allium, 2–3 ft.; purple-pink egg-shaped flowerheads; naturalizes well
* *A. triquetrum* Three-cornered leek, 1 ft.; loose clusters of dangling white, bell-shaped flowers; naturalizes well

A. karataviense

Star of Persia

Begonia

Begonia Tuberhybrida hybrids
Tuberous begonia

Spectacular plants for shade, tuberous begonias produce their big, splashy blossoms in brilliant warm colors and show them off against contrasting dark green leaves. The flowers of various cultivars are formed similarly to camellias, roses, or carnations.

'Apricot Lace'

Blooming Time: Midsummer to fall.

Hardiness: Zones 10 and 11; elsewhere, dig and store indoors over winter.

Height: 8 inches to 1½ feet.

Light: Partial to medium shade; need shade at least part of the day.

Depth and Spacing: Set the top of the tubers at soil level, 10 to 15 inches apart.

Soil: Well-drained, fertile, humusy, deeply dug.

Moisture: Even but not soggy.

Garden Uses: Tuberous begonias grow and bloom beautifully in shady or partly shady gardens. Many are cascading or trailing and work wonderfully in pots, tubs,

Red and yellow begonias mix with browallias in a shady garden bed.

window boxes, or hanging baskets on shady porches or patios.

Comments: Begonias need a long growing season; if you live in a cold climate, start the tubers indoors in February or March, as shown on page 75. Plant or transplant outdoors when all danger of frost has passed, and fertilize monthly with an all-purpose fertilizer until blooming begins. Switch to a low-nitrogen fertilizer or compost once plants have flowers. Because the flowers are large and heavy, all but the cascading types usually need staking.

In cold climates, dig begonia tubers after the first frost; in warm areas, wait until the leaves yellow and start to turn brown at the end of the season. After digging, spread out newly dug tubers and let them dry in the sun for a few days. Then cut off the stems an inch above the tops of the tubers. Shake off the soil, lay the tubers in a shallow box or tray, and cover them with peat moss or dry sand. Pack tubers of the same flower color together, and label the boxes so you know what you're planting in spring. The best storage temperature is 40° to 50°F.

Recommended Cultivars:
• Camellia-flowered begonias, red, pink, yellow, white flowers shaped like camellias
• Picotee, Crispa, and Marginata hybrids; edged in red, pink, orange
• Cascade begonias, trailing habit; bloom in red, pink, yellow, white, mixed pastel shades
• Non Stop begonias, double flowers; all summer; red, pink, orange, white
• Carnation (Fimbriata group) begonias, fringed petals in red, orange, yellow, white

SMART TIP

Storing Begonia Tubers
Store tubers over winter, concave side up, in a single layer in dry peat moss or sand.

Hardening Off

Harden off plants by exposing them gradually to the outside.

Convallaria

Convallaria majalis
Lily-of-the-valley

Lily-of-the-valley is a carefree perennial that grows from small, pointed, bulblike structures known as "pips." The waxy bell-shaped little flowers dance along small slender stems for an all-too-brief couple of weeks each year, perfuming the air with an unmistakable sweet fragrance.

In autumn, lily-of-the-valley leaves turn yellow before turning brown. Placed in a rock garden, as they are here, their color adds vibrancy to the autumn landscape palette.

The large, elliptical leaves, about 8 inches high, grow from the base of the plant; they remain until late summer, when they begin to turn brown and die back.

Lily-of-the-valley

Blooming Time: Late spring.

Hardiness: Zones 3 to 9.

Height: 8 inches to 1 foot.

Depth and Spacing: 2 inches deep, 4 inches apart.

Light: Filtered sun to light shade.

Soil: Well-drained, humusy, average fertility; tolerates a range of soils.

Moisture: Average to even.

Garden Uses: Lily-of-the-valley likes to spread, so it is not a good addition to an orderly bed or border. Instead, give it a place of its own along a sidewalk or massed in a corner of the yard, or grow it as a ground cover in an informal shady or woodland garden.

The fragrant flowers are good for cutting and useful as fillers in bouquets and arrangements, although they only last a few days in the vase if cut when fully open. To get the longest life in the vase, cut when the topmost buds on a stem have turned white, but before the flowers open. If you have cut the stem low enough that the white base of the stem is visible, recut the stem to remove the white portion. Condition the flowers before arranging them by standing the stems in a container of water nearly up to the base of the flowers for several hours.

Comments: Lily-of-the-valley is too invasive for some people. If it grows where you don't want it, you'll need to dig it up to remove it. The leaves tend to turn straggly and brown around the edges in a hot, dry summer. Trim off ragged or brown leaves if necessary to keep plants looking neat and to avoid disease. If you can't accommodate its foibles in your yard but still want to enjoy the flowers, try forcing the pips indoors in winter.

Recommended Cultivars:
• 'Fortin's Giant', to 12 in.; white, large flowers
• 'Plena', double white flowers;
• *C. majalis* var. *rosea*, pink blooms
• 'Albostriata', leaves with thin, creamy white stripes running along their length, with white flowers
• 'Aureovariegata', white flowers and leaves with yellow stripes
• 'Hardwick Hall', broad leaves with narrow pale green margins and large flowers

C. majalis var. rosea

Ripe seedpods show off colorful display in autumn.

Crocus

Crocus species and cultivars

There are two groups of crocuses—spring bloomers and fall bloomers. The earliest spring species flower in late winter and early spring. The larger Dutch hybrids also bloom in early spring, but a bit later than many of the species. Autumn crocuses, as the name implies, send up their welcome blossoms in fall. All crocuses have chalice-shaped blossoms and narrow, grassy leaves. The color range of the flowers includes various shades of purple, lavender, yellow, and white, and some are striped or bicolored. Most autumn crocuses flower in shades of purple.

Blooming Time: Late winter to spring or in autumn, depending on species and cultivar.

Early Spring bloomer

Hardiness: Zones 4 to 8, varies with species.

Height: 4 to 6 inches.

Depth and Spacing: 3 to 4 inches deep, 3 inches apart.

Light: Full sun.

Soil: Well-drained; average fertility.

Moisture: Average.

Garden Uses: Crocuses welcome spring. Plant them in the front of beds and borders, in containers, and along a path or sidewalk. Or let them naturalize in a part of the lawn you can leave unmowed for eight weeks after they finish blooming.

The lilacs, lavenders, and purples of autumn crocuses offer a lovely counterpoint to the warm, earthy tones of orange, russet, gold, bronze, and beige of the mums, pumpkins, and ornamental grasses that are so abundant at this time of year.

Comments: Wherever you plant crocuses, plant lots of them, and give them room to spread. Crocuses love the sun; they thrive when their dormant bulbs can bake in soil warmed by it during the summer. When the plants become crowded after several years, they will produce fewer flowers. Revive the planting by lifting and dividing the corms in fall or late spring after the foliage has died

'Purple Giant'

back. Plant bulbs for spring bloomers in autumn and those for autumn bloomers in late summer. Stigmas of the fall-bloomer *C. sativus* are the spice, saffron.

Recommended Cultivars:
Spring bloomers:
• snow crocuses (*C. chrysanthus* cultivars), usual range of crocus colors plus some unusual blue-and-yellow and red-brown-and-yellow bicolors
• tommies (*C. tommasinianus*), several shades of purple, red-purple, lavender
• Dutch crocus (*C. vernus*), larger flowers in a pretty range of crocus colors; most widely grown type because they are easy to grow, dependable, inexpensive
Autumn bloomers:
• saffron crocus (*C. sativus*), purple, red-orange stigmata
• *C. goulimyi*, warm climates; pale to deep purple
• *C. kotschyanus*, cold, damp climates; pale lilac with darker purple veins and a soft yellow throat
• *C. speciosus*, blooms early; good for gardens where winter snow comes early; lilac-purple

Buying Corms

Purchase unsprouted corms whenever possible. Corms that have sprouted before planting will be weakened and may not bloom their best the first year.

Planting Crocus Bulbs
Plant crocuses in large groups for maximum visual impact. Space corms 3 to 4 inches apart for best growth.

Convallaria, Crocus

3 Introducing Bulbs

Dahlia

Dahlia x *pinnata* cultivars

Members of this genus of tender tuberous plants have been extensively bred into thousands of flamboyant, large-flowered cultivars. The flowers resemble chrysanthemums, and they come in a wide range of warm colors, flower forms, and sizes. The American Dahlia Society recognizes 17 different flower classes: formal decorative, informal decorative, semi-cactus, straight cactus, incurved cactus, laciniated, ball, miniature ball, pompom, waterlily, peony, anemone, collarette, single, mignon single, orchid, and novelty (forms that don't fit into any of the other categories).

'Alabaster'

Blooming Time: Late summer into autumn; in many areas they peak in September.

Hardiness: Zones 7 to 11; elsewhere dig tubers in fall and store indoors over winter.

Height: 10 inches to 7 feet.

Depth and Spacing: 6 inches deep, 2 to 3 feet apart.

Light: Full sun (at least six hours of sun a day to produce the best flowers).

Soil: Loose, rich, loamy soil with good fertility and excellent drainage.

Moisture: Even; plants like lots of moisture but do not tolerate soggy soil.

Garden Uses: Plant dahlias in groups in beds and borders. Shorter cultivars go in the front of the garden and very tall ones in the back.

Comments: Plant dahlia tubers in spring as soon as the danger of frost is past. In very cool climates (Zones 3 to 5), start them indoors in pots to get earlier flowers. All but the dwarf cultivars will need staking. To avoid damaging the tuberous roots, set the stakes in place before planting.

When planting, lay the root horizontally in the hole with the eye, or growing point, facing upward and toward the stake. Cover the tuber with 2 to 3 inches of soil, leaving a depression. As the shoots grow, gradually fill in around them with more soil, until just a very shallow depression remains; this will hold water for the plant.

Allow only the one or two of the strongest shoots to

Deadheading
Dahlias respond to regular deadheading by prolonging their bloomtime by several extra weeks. Make it a habit to deadhead every three or four days.

develop on each plant—cut back the rest at ground level. From early summer until autumn, cultivate lightly once a week to keep the soil well-aerated. About the middle of August, give the flowers a nutrient boost. Scratch a handful of all-purpose fertilizer into the soil around each plant, or mulch with compost and then water with a mixture of liquid seaweed and fish emulsion.

In warm parts of Zone 7 and Zones 8 to 11, dahlias can overwinter under a thick mulch. Elsewhere, after a heavy frost has blackened the plants in autumn, cut back the stems to 4 inches above ground level. Dig up the clumps of tubers and store them indoors over the winter in dry peat moss in a cool (40° to 50°F), dry place. Divide the clumps before replanting in spring.

Recommended Cultivars: Choose cultivars based on your preferences for height, flower form, and color. All present-day cultivars perform well under a variety of circumstances.

Dahlia Classifications

Dahlias are classed by the appearance of their flowers. Some common classes include:

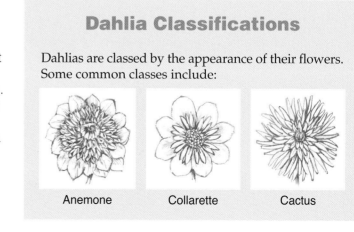

| Anemone | Collarette | Cactus |

Gladiolus

Gladiolus x *hortulanus* cultivars

The bold, brightly colored flower spikes of gladiolus are a familiar summertime sight in backyards, flower stands, and farmer's markets. The color range of today's gladiolus hybrids includes practically every warm color imaginable plus various shades of lavender, an unusual lime green, white, and bicolors. The flowers bloom along sturdy upright stems; plants have stiff, sword-shaped leaves.

Gladiolus

Blooming Time: Early summer to fall, if planted in succession.

Hardiness: Zones 8 to 11; in other zones, dig and store indoors over winter.

Height: 2 to 6 feet.

Depth and Spacing: Large corms (an inch or larger), 6 to 8 inches deep, medium-size corms (½ to 1 inch) 4 to 5 inches deep, and smaller corms 3 inches deep; plant all sizes of corms 6 to 8 inches apart.

Light: Full sun.

Soil: Deep, loose, rich soil.

Moisture: Even.

Garden Uses: Gladiolus are classics for cutting gardens. Put the tall, spiky plants in the back of display gardens.

Comments: Gladiolus is a fairly demanding plant when it comes to nutrient and moisture levels. To ensure high soil fertility, incorporate plenty of organic matter into the bed and mix some gypsum, rock phosphate, and all-purpose fertilizer in the bottom of the planting holes or trenches. When the flower spike appears, make sure the plants get plenty of water. During dry weather water deeply every two or three days.

For a succession of bloom, plant gladiolus in batches two weeks apart from just after the last frost until midsummer. This ensures that some plants will be blooming from midsummer until early fall.

Gladiolus spikes grow quite tall and often need staking. There are also smaller-growing miniature cultivars on the market.

At the end of the growing season, dig the corms. Even warm-climate gardeners often lift them because they can become weedy if left in place. Unlike spring bulbs, gladiolus corms can be dug before the leaves die; you can start lifting the frost-tender corms a month to six weeks after the plants have finished blooming. As soon as you dig the corms, cut off the leaves to the top of the corm. Destroy the old foliage because it can harbor pests and diseases that will winter over and attack plants the following year. Spread the corms in an open container to dry; separate the smaller bulblets when you can pull them off easily. Store them over the winter in a cool, dry, well-ventilated place. If you live in a warm climate, place the corms in cold storage to ensure that they enter dormancy.

Recommended Cultivars: Today's gladiolus cultivars perform well under a variety of circumstances. Choose cultivars based on your color and height preferences. In addition to the fancy cultivars, try the following species:
• *G. byzantinus*, to 3 ft.; pink, white, burgundy, rosy purple with white stripe
• *G. cardinalis*, to 3 ft.; red blooms marked with white
• *G. nanus*, to 2 ft.; hardy; mulch well for winter in Zones 3 to 5; flowers in red, pink, white, bicolors
• *G. tristis*, to 2 ft.; fragrant white flowers streaked with purple, open at night

Storing Gladiolus Corms

1. Dig corms in fall, before frost, and cut off the leaves.

2. Brush all loose soil from the corms with your fingers.

3. Dip corms in a 10 percent solution of chlorine bleach and fresh water.

4. Dry and store in a single layer in a cardboard box.

Hyacinthus

Hyacinthus orientalis cultivars
Hyacinth

Most of the hyacinths found in American gardens are hybrid bulbs that were grown in the Netherlands and bred from the common garden species, *H. orientalis*. Their star-shaped flowers cluster together in a dense, fat spike at the top of a thick stem. The color range has expanded beyond the traditional pink, white, and blue to include red, yellow, apricot, and deep purple. The intense, sweet fragrance of the flowers provokes strong reactions—some people love the scent and others detest it, but it's hard to ignore.

Blooming Time: Mid-spring.

Hardiness: Zones 3 to 9.

Height: 10 inches to 1 foot.

Depth and Spacing: 6 inches deep, 6 to 9 inches apart.

Light: Full sun.

Soil: Well-drained.

Moisture: Average.

Garden Uses: Hyacinths aren't easy to integrate into a garden with other flowers, but you can plant them in groups in beds and borders. They also grow well in containers. They're easy to force indoors in winter. (See below.)

'Jan Bos'

Comments: To overwinter hyacinths in Zones 3 and 4, mulch them well after the top inch of the soil has frozen. Gardeners in Zones 3 and 4 can also plant the bulbs in very early spring and dig them in fall like dahlias and gladiolus. Store them over the winter in a cardboard box filled with peat moss; place them in a single layer and cover with more peat moss before placing them in the dark.

The stems may need staking to support the weight of the flowers in the first year; in subsequent years, the flower spikes tend to be less heavy and dense.

Recommended Cultivars:
- 'Blue Jacket', deep violet-blue • 'Bolero', apricot-pink
- 'Champagne', bluish pink • 'City of Haarlem', yellow
- 'Distinction', unusually slender, open flower clusters in a deep red-purple • 'Hollyhock', double; bright red
- 'Gipsy Queen', apricot-orange • 'Jan Bos', carmine
- 'Lady Derby', rosy pink • 'L'Innocence', white
- 'Peter Stuyvesant', purple-blue • 'Pink Pearl', deep pink
- 'Sheila', pale pink • 'Sky Jacket', light blue
- 'Blue Giant', light blue • 'Woodstock', purple-red.

Planting for Forcing Hyacinths

1. For forcing indoors, place several bulbs in a 4-inch pot, ½ inch apart.

2. Cover the bulbs with porous potting mix and water well; then place in cold storage.

Heirloom hyacinth cultivars

I. reticulata

I. xiphium

Iris

Iris species and cultivars
Bulbous irises

Irises have long been favorite garden flowers. Most gardeners are familiar with the lovely bearded irises a favorite perennial that blooms in late spring and grows from rhizomes. But there are also smaller irises that grow from bulbs and flower earlier in spring. The earliest to bloom outdoors are the bulbous *I. histrioides*, *I. danfordiae*, and *I. reticulata*; these are sometimes called dwarf or rock garden irises because their small stature suits them to planting in a rock garden. All of these have the classic iris form with standards and falls. *I. histrioides* comes in shades of blue and purple, some with contrasting yellow flushes and deeper blue markings. *I. danfordiae* is bright yellow. *I. reticulata*, the best known of the three, is available in several blue and purple shades as well as yellow, white, and bicolors.

Another bulbous iris is the later blooming Dutch iris (*I. xiphium* x *I. tingitana*), which has slender, graceful flowers in shades of blue, purple, pink, and white, along with some lovely bicolored combinations. Dutch irises have a limited hardiness range and don't do well in either cold climates or the lower South.

Blooming Time: *I. histrioides*, *I. danfordiae*, and *I. reticulata*, late winter to early spring; Dutch iris, late spring to early summer.

Hardiness: *I. histrioides*, *I. danfordiae*, and *I. reticulata*, Zones 5 to 9; Dutch iris, Zones 6 to 9.

I. danfordiae

Height: Dwarf, 4 to 6 inches; Dutch iris, 1½ to 2 feet.

Depth and Spacing: Dwarf species, 4 inches deep, 4 to 5 inches apart; Dutch iris, 6 inches deep, 6 inches apart.

Light: Full sun.

Soil: Well-drained, average fertility.

Moisture: Average; dwarf species can't tolerate soggy soil, especially in summer.

Garden Uses: Plant dwarf irises in large groups in the front of beds and borders, in the rock garden, or in containers. They are easy to force indoors for winter bloom.

Dutch irises are lovely in the middle ground of beds and borders and make good companions for roses and peonies. They are long-lasting as cut flowers.

Comments: Plant dwarf species in fall. Many dwarf irises are fragrant, making them delightful when forced indoors.

Plant Dutch irises in spring in cool climates and fall in warm areas. They usually need a good winter mulch in Zone 6. You can also dig the bulbs in fall and store them indoors over winter as you would dahlias or gladiolus.

To enjoy Dutch iris as cut flowers, cut the stems when the buds are plump and let them unfurl indoors.

Recommended Cultivars:
I. reticulata:
• 'Springtime', sky blue flowers
• 'Harmony', blue flowers with yellow and white markings
• 'Ida', blue falls with lighter blue standards
• 'J.S. Dijt', purple standards with red-purple falls
• 'Natasha', palest blue-white • 'Pixie', blue-black
I. histrioides:
• 'George', deep purple
• 'Katharine Hodgkin', blue standards with greenish falls blotched with yellow
• 'Major', deep-blue flowers on vigorous plants
Dutch iris:
• 'Blue Magic', blue-violet • 'Sky Beauty', light blue
• 'Marquette', white standards with yellow falls
• 'Silvery Beauty', pale blue-and-white
• 'Bronze Beauty', bronze with gold splotch on falls
• 'Cream Beauty', white standards; yellow and orange falls
• 'Telstar', violet standards with blue falls
• 'White Wedgwood', white
• 'Golden Harvest', yellow
• 'Rosario', pink

I. reticulata bulbs

Lilium

Lilium species and cultivars
Lily

Unlike daylilies, with which they are sometimes confused, true lilies have traditionally been considered hard to grow. Yet today's hybrids are sturdier than their predecessors and bloom beautifully if you give them the growing conditions they prefer. The mostly trumpet-shaped flowers come in a range of colors, sizes, and blooming times. They grow on tall, straight stems lined with narrow, pointed leaves.

Blooming Time: Summer.

Hardiness: Zones 4 to 8.

Height: 2 to 8 feet, depending on species or cultivar.

Depth and Spacing: 4 to 8 inches deep (or three times as deep as the bulbs are tall), 1 to 1½ feet apart.

Light: Filtered or not-quite full sun.

Soil: Light and loamy, with absolutely perfect drainage.

Moisture: Evenly moist before and during bloom, average afterwards.

Garden Uses: Plant lilies in groups in mixed beds and borders or grow them in a cutting garden.

Comments: Try to plant lilies in a spot with filtered sun for most of the day; full sun bleaches out the colors of some lily flowers. Most lily bulbs are planted in fall, but some of the late-blooming types can be planted in spring. Gardeners in Zones 9 to 11 can dig and refrigerate the bulbs for two months before planting in spring.

The plants are heavy feeders and benefit from one to

'Herald Angel Yellow' trumpet lily

two applications of an all-purpose fertilizer in spring. Also topdress with compost or leaf mold to make sure their soil is rich in organic matter.

During dry weather, water the plants once a week until they bloom. After they finish flowering, the plants like drier conditions. Lilies cannot tolerate moisture standing around the bulbs. They also do not like hot soil, so you need to either mulch them or overplant them with annuals or ground covers to shade the roots and help keep the soil cool.

Many lilies grow tall—6 feet or more—and need to be staked. It is a good idea to stake all cultivars that grow taller than 3 feet. The stakes need to be far enough away from the plants so that they don't touch the bulbs. For appearance's sake, insert the stakes just before the first flowers open. To prevent the stems from being damaged as they move with the breeze, attach them to the stakes loosely, with ties that form figure eights that cross between the stem and stake.

Every few years, when the plants become crowded, lift and divide the bulbs. After the plants have finished blooming and the foliage has died back in fall, carefully dig up the clumps, leaving as many of the roots intact as you can. Very gently separate the bulbs, and replant them immediately. Keep the bulbs out of the soil for only the briefest possible time so they do not dry out.

Lilies propagate themselves with small bulblets and, as shown on page 87, aboveground bulbils and seeds.

Recommended Cultivars: Many lilies are available, both hybrids and species. A few of the best include:
Asiatic Hybrids (bloom in early summer):
• 'Connecticut King', 2½–3 ft.; golden yellow
• 'Coral Sunrise', 3–4 ft.; coral-pink, flushed peach-yellow
• 'Enchantment', 3–4 ft.; red-orange
• 'Luxor', 3–4 ft.; light yellow flushed with apricot
• 'Marissa', 2–3 ft. peach flushed with apricot and gold
• 'Shirley', 3–4 ft.; white brushed with pink at center
• 'Sorbet', 3–4 ft.; white with burgundy edges and spots

'Casa Blanca' oriental lily

Oriental Hybrids (large flowers in late summer, most with reflexed petals, often fragrant):
• 'Blushing Pink', 5 ft.; soft pink
• 'Casa Blanca', 4 ft. large, white, very fragrant
• 'Dolce Vita', 3–4 ft.; rose-pink
• 'Emmely', 3–5 ft.; pink with white edges and a deeper pink stripe down the center of the petals
• 'Mediterranee', 2½–3½ ft.; rich pink
• 'Pink Paramount', 3– 3½ ft.; clear pink, fragrant
• 'Sans Souci', 2 ft. crimson. white edges and darker spots
• 'Silver Elegance', 4–5 ft.; white with red spots
• 'Star Gazer', 2½–3 ft.; deep reddish pink with white edges
Trumpet Lilies (derived from Asiatic Hybrids, very fragrant, trumpet shaped):
• 'Herald Angel Yellow', 3–5 ft.; yellow, dark yellow throat
• *L. speciosum* var. *rubrum*, 3–5 feet, late summer, reflexed petals, light crimson-and-white with crimson spots
• *L. tigrinum* tiger lily, 2–5 ft.; mid- to late summer, reflexed petals, orange with dark spots

'Connecticut King' Asiatic lily

Tiger lily

Propagating Lilies

1. Propagate Asiatic lilies by dividing them in fall or collecting and planting bulbils when they form in leaf axils.

2. Collect seeds of trumpet lilies when seedpods are dry. Plants grown from seed will combine traits of parent plants.

3. Propagate tiger lilies by digging, separating, and replanting small bullets that form underground. They grow to blooming size in three years.

Narcissus

Narcissus species and cultivars
Daffodil

There are many kinds of daffodils. For simplicity, the plants can be divided into two major groups—the small-growing species and their derivatives (which are grown in rock gardens and in the front of the garden), and the vast group of larger cultivars and hybrids.

Daffodils can be grown in most climates, but different types perform better in different places. In very cold climates, small-cupped, poeticus, and jonquil types work best. In Zones 8 and warmer, try small-cupped, jonquilla, triandrus, and tazetta types. Stay away from late-blooming cultivars if you live in a warm climate, because the weather will be too hot for them when they bloom.

Blooming Time: Early to mid-spring.

'King Alfred'

'Edna Earl'

Hardiness: Varies with species and cultivar.

Height: 6 inches to 1½ feet.

Depth and Spacing: Small species and cultivars 3 to 5 inches deep, 4 to 5 inches apart; larger ones 6 inches deep, 6 inches apart.

Light: Full sun to partial shade.

Soil: Well-drained, rich in organic matter.

Moisture: Evenly moist during growth and blooming, average the rest of the year.

Garden Uses: Daffodils are delightful in beds and borders and also grow well in containers. Plant them along paths, tuck them into foundation plantings—put them wherever you'll see their welcome flowers in spring.

Smaller triandrus and cyclamineus types are good additions to rock gardens and make bright spots in a woodland garden.

For an early taste of spring, force various types of daffodils and some of the delightful paperwhite narcissus into bloom indoors in winter.

Comments: Plant bulbs in fall, at least a month before you expect the first frost. Feed the plants once a year with compost or an all-purpose fertilizer.

If you want the plants to naturalize but don't want to divide them often, plant them deeper than normal—they won't spread as quickly and will be maintenance-free for a longer time. When in doubt, plant deeper rather than shallower.

In beds and borders, daffodils need to be lifted and divided every four years or so. Dig the bulbs after the foliage dies back in late spring or early summer. Let them dry in the shade. Don't divide them until the offsets break off easily; otherwise you risk damaging the basal plates. You can replant the divided bulbs right away or store them until autumn in a cool, dry, well-ventilated place.

Recommended Cultivars: There are many excellent narcissus species and cultivars. See the box, opposite, for a sampling.

Dividing Daffodils

1. Dig daffodil bulbs for division after the leaves die back in late spring. Pull off the bulblets around the bulb's base.

2. Replant the bulbs immediately, at the correct depth and spacing, or store and replant in fall.

Types of Daffodils

Narcissus and daffodils are divided into 12 groups or divisions according to their flower type.

■ **Division 1:** Trumpet daffodils have one flower to a stem. The central trumpet, or *corona*, is as long as or longer than the length of the outer petals (the *perianth*). The flowers may be all yellow, all white, or bicolored. Good cultivars include: 'King Alfred', all yellow; 'Mount Hood', creamy white; 'Empress of Ireland', pure white; 'Arctic Gold', all yellow; 'Rinjveld's Early Sensation', yellow, very early blooming; 'General Patton', white perianth with yellow trumpet.

■ **Division 2:** Large-cupped daffodils have large coronas, but they aren't as long as those of the trumpets. Stems bear only one flower. The flowers usually have a yellow or white perianth and a colored (often orange) cup, though some are all white or yellow. Good cultivars include: 'Accent', white perianth with salmon-pink cup; 'Roseworthy', white with orangy pink cup; 'Salome', white with pinkish yellow cup; 'Ice Follies', white with yellow cup that turns white as it matures; 'Carlton', all yellow.

■ **Division 3:** Short-cupped daffodils also have only one flower to a stem. In these, the corona is smaller and substantially shorter than the perianth. Good cultivars include: 'Barrett Browning', white perianth with orange cup; 'Polar Ice', all white, fragrant; 'Segovia', white with yellow cup.

■ **Division 4:** Double daffodils can grow with one or more flowers to a stem. Doubling can occur in the perianth, the corona, or in both. Good cultivars include: 'Acropolis', white perianth, corona flushed orange in center; 'Erlicheer', clusters of fragrant, ivory-yellow flowers; 'Cheerfulness', clusters of fragrant, creamy white or yellow flowers; 'Ice King', white perianth with creamy yellow ruffled cup; 'Tahiti', yellow perianth and corona with orange in center.

■ **Division 5:** Triandrus daffodils usually bear two or more pendent flowers on each stem. The perianth petals are reflexed. Good cultivars include: 'Thalia', white, fragrant; 'Hawera', light yellow, fragrant.

■ **Division 6:** Cyclamineus daffodils bear only one flower to a stem and are distinguished by their highly reflexed petals. Good cultivars include: 'February Gold', all yellow; 'Jack Snipe', white petals with yellow cup; 'Jenny', white petals, corona opens pale yellow and turns white.

N. cyclamineus

■ **Division 7:** Jonquilla daffodils, the jonquils, have one to three flowers on each stem. The flowers are fragrant and petals in the perianth spread out. The corona can be small, so some of these resemble the small-cupped types. Good cultivars include: 'Baby Moon', pale yellow, miniature; 'Suzy', red-orange cup, yellow perianth; 'Quail', bronzy yellow.

■ **Division 8:** Tazetta types usually carry 3 to 20 highly fragrant blooms on each stem. The perianth petals spread out, and the corona is short. Good cultivars include: 'Geranium', white with orange cup, very fragrant; 'Cragford', white with orange cup, fragrant and *N. papyraceus*, paperwhite narcissus, not hardy north of Zone 9 but easily forced, clusters of white, fragrant blooms.

■ **Division 9:** The Poeticus group includes both species and hybrids, all of them recognizable by their large white perianth petals and contrasting small, flat corona with a green or yellow center and a red rim. The flowers are fragrant. Look for: 'Actaea', white perianth, yellow cup edged in red, fragrant, tolerates moist locations.

■ **Division 10:** Species, Wild Forms, and Natural Hybrids can be single or double, fragrant or unscented. Their unifying charactristic is that they were discovered growing in the wild. Look for: *N. bulbocodium* var. *conspicuus*, hoop petticoat daffodil, yellow, funnel-shaped flowers.

■ **Division 11:** Split Corona daffodils have a corona that is split for about half its length or more, giving the bloom a somewhat flattened appearance. Good cultivars include: 'Broadway Star', orange corona, white perianth; 'Lemon Beauty', lemon yellow corona, white perianth.

■ **Division 12:** Miscellaneous daffodils include those that do not fit into one of the other divisions, such as 'Tête-à-Tête' and cultivars of *N. bulbocodium*.

Tulipa

Tulipa species and cultivars
Tulip

Tulips have cup-shaped blossoms with pointed petals. The petals of some types remain cupped, but in others they open wide like stars. Tulips bloom in many warm shades as well as purples, white, and bicolors. Flowers top straight, slender stems that rise above oblong, pointed leaves of varying widths.

Thousands of tulip cultivars are available. You'll find a wide selection of heights, colors, and blooming times and several different flower forms. Botanists have divided tulips into 15 divisions, as described in the box on the facing page. When you buy bulbs, you'll find that most nurseries also use these categories to describe their stock.

Unfortunately, many hybrid tulips are not reliably perennial, or are short-lived, especially in warm climates. So many gardeners prefer to treat them as annuals, digging and discarding the bulbs when they finish blooming and replanting the space with summer annuals. Species tulips often last longer in the garden.

Parrot tulips

Blooming Time: Mid- to late spring.

Height: 4 inches to 2½ feet.

Depth and Spacing: 3 to 6 inches deep (deeper to encourage hybrids to rebloom in subsequent years); 3 to 6 inches apart. Planting depth and spacing vary with the type and size of bulb. Follow the directions that come with the bulbs you buy.

Hardiness: Zones 4 to 7 or 8.

Light: Full sun.

Soil: Deep, rich, well-drained soil with a neutral to slightly alkaline pH.

Moisture: Average.

Garden Uses: Plant tulips in groups in beds and borders, in cottage gardens, and along paths and walkways. Smaller species and hybrids, such as the Kaufmanniana hybrids, are at home in rock gardens, too. And, as described on page 84, tulips can be forced for winter flowers indoors.

Comments: Hybrid tulips are often not reliably perennials, so many gardeners prefer to treat them as annuals even where they are hardy, pulling them up when they finish blooming. If you wish to treat your tulips as perennials, deadhead the flowers after they fade, and leave the foliage in place until it yellows and dries. In warm climates, treat them as annuals, or dig the bulbs after they finish blooming and keep them refrigerated until you replant them in fall.

Recommended Cultivars: There are many good cultivars. For suggestions, see the box, opposite.

Protecting Tulips from Rodents

1. Rodents love tulips; line planting areas with screen cages where they're a problem.

2. Dig the soil to the correct depth, and line the bottom and sides with metal screening.

3. Set the bulbs in a layer of soil at the bottom of the cage, at the correct depth and spacing.

4. Cover with soil and water well.

Types of Tulips

- **Division 1: Single Early** tulips, the first group, bloom early (along with hyacinths), are usually short-stemmed (10 to 18 inches tall), and come in a range of colors. Good cultivars include: 'Apricot Beauty', salmon-pink; 'Beauty Queen', apricot-rose; 'Bellona', yellow; 'Christmas Dream', reddish pink.

- **Division 2: Double Early** tulips bloom slightly later than the single early, are 10 to 12 inches tall, and are double in form. Good cultivars include: 'Monte Carlo', yellow; 'Peach Blossom', rosy pink; 'Schoonoord', white.

- **Division 3: Triumph** hybrids bloom right in the middle of the tulip season, in mid-spring. Plants range from 16 to 24 inches tall and are mostly red, white, and shades of pink. Many of the flowers have a second color flamed onto the petals. Good cultivars include: 'Arabian Mystery', deep purple with white edge; 'Cream Perfection', pale yellow; 'Bastogne', deep red; 'Golden Melody', buttercup yellow; 'Ile de France', deep red.

- **Division 4: Darwin** hybrids are large-flowered plants that range in height from 22 to 34 inches tall. They bloom in mid-spring in a range of bright colors and often have a black blotch at the base of the petals. Good cultivars include: 'Apeldoorn', bright red; 'Cream Jewel', creamy white; 'Daydream', opens yellow, turns apricot-orange; 'Elizabeth Arden', purple pink to salmon pink; 'General Eisenhower', rich red; 'Ivory Floradale', opens pale yellow, turns ivory; 'Orange Sun', bright orange.; 'Pink Impression', pink and rose blend; 'President Kennedy', yellow with red.

- **Division 5: Single Late** tulips used to be called cottage tulips. This group also includes what used to be called Darwin tulips, which are not the same as the newer Darwin hybrids. Ranging in height from 9 to 32 inches, they have pointed petals and long stems. Good cultivars include: 'Aristocrat', purplish rose with light edge; 'Bleu Aimable', bluish lilac; 'Dreamland', purplish red flamed with cream.

- **Division 6: Lily-flowered** tulips have pointed petals and a gracefully curving shape. They range from 20 to 30 inches tall and come in colors representing the entire tulip range, except for dark purples and maroons. They hold well in the vase. Good cultivars include: 'Ballade', purple-rose with broad white edge; 'Ballerina', light yellow flamed with scarlet; 'Elegant Lady', ivory with pale purple-pink edge; 'White Triumphator', white.

- **Division 7: Fringed** tulips have petals that are cut into fringe at the edges. Plants range from 10 to 26 inches tall and bloom late. Good cultivars include: 'Burgundy Lace', wine red; 'Fringed Elegance', primrose yellow with thin red edging; 'Swan Wings', white.

- **Division 8: Viridiflora** tulips have green stripes or markings on their petals. Plants are 10 to 20 inches high and bloom late. Good cultivars include: 'Golden Artist', golden yellow feathered with green; 'Greenland', soft rose striped with green.

- **Division 9: Rembrandt** tulips are no longer commercially available.

- **Division 10: Parrot** tulips are distinguished by fringed, curled, twisted, or narrow petals. Many of the large flowers are streaked with a contrasting color and sometimes droop on the stems. Plants are 12 to 30 inches tall and flower late. Good cultivars include: 'Apricot Parrot', apricot tinged with yellow, green, pink, and white; 'Black Parrot', deep purple-black.

- **Division 11: Double Late** or **Peony** tulips have multiple petals and hold in the garden for long periods of time. They range from 16 to 24 inches tall and bloom late. Good cultivars include: 'Angélique', soft pink edged in cream; 'Blue Diamond', deep violet-purple.

- **Division 12: Kaufmanniana** hybrids are sometimes called water-lily tulips because of their open habit. They bloom about mid-spring. Their foliage is often mottled or striped, and they grow to about a foot tall. Good cultivars include: 'Ancilla', rosy red and soft pink, white interior; 'Gaiety', white with broad red stripe.

- **Division 13: Fosteriana** tulips bloom in mid-spring. The plants grow a foot to almost a foot and a half tall, the foliage can be mottled or striped, and the flowers are quite large. Good cultivars include: 'Orange Emperor', rich orange; 'Pink Emperor', reddish pink.

- **Division 14: Greigii** hybrids grow from 8 inches to 1¼ tall and have foliage that is streaked and mottled with purple. They bloom in mid-spring, after Kaufmanniana hybrids. Good cultivars include: 'Donna Bella', carmine with wide ivory edging and interior; 'Garden Show', rich red.

- **Division 15: Other Species.** Tulips that don't fit into any of the above divisions are classified as Division XV plants.

zone maps

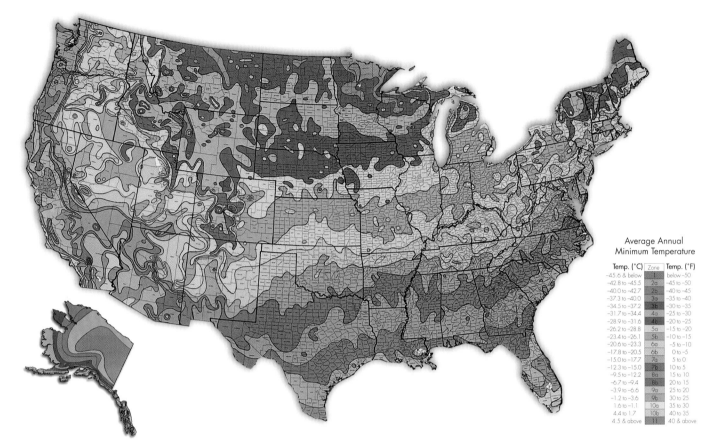

Average Annual Minimum Temperature		
Temp. (°C)	**Zone**	**Temp. (°F)**
−45.6 & below	1	below −50
−42.8 to −45.5	2a	−45 to −50
−40.0 to −42.7	2b	−40 to −45
−37.3 to −40.0	3a	−35 to −40
−34.5 to −37.2	3b	−30 to −35
−31.7 to −34.4	4a	−25 to −30
−28.9 to −31.6	4b	−20 to −25
−26.2 to −28.8	5a	−15 to −20
−23.4 to −26.1	5b	−10 to −15
−20.6 to −23.3	6a	−5 to −10
−17.8 to −20.5	6b	0 to −5
−15.0 to −17.7	7a	5 to 0
−12.3 to −15.0	7b	10 to 5
−9.5 to −12.2	8a	15 to 10
−6.7 to −9.4	8b	20 to 15
−3.9 to −6.6	9a	25 to 20
−1.2 to −3.6	9b	30 to 25
1.6 to −1.1	10a	35 to 30
4.4 to 1.7	10b	40 to 35
4.5 & above	11	40 & above

The USDA Hardiness Map divides North America into 11 zones according to average minimum winter temperatures. Hardiness zones are used to identify regions to which plants are suited based on their cold tolerance, which is what "hardiness" means. Many factors, such as elevation and moisture level, come into play when determining whether a plant is suitable for your region. Local climates may vary from what is shown on this map. Contact your local Cooperative Extension Service for recommendations for your area.

Plant Hardiness Zones

0a	4a
0b	4b
1a	5a
1b	5b
2a	6a
2b	6b
3a	7a
3b	7b
	8a

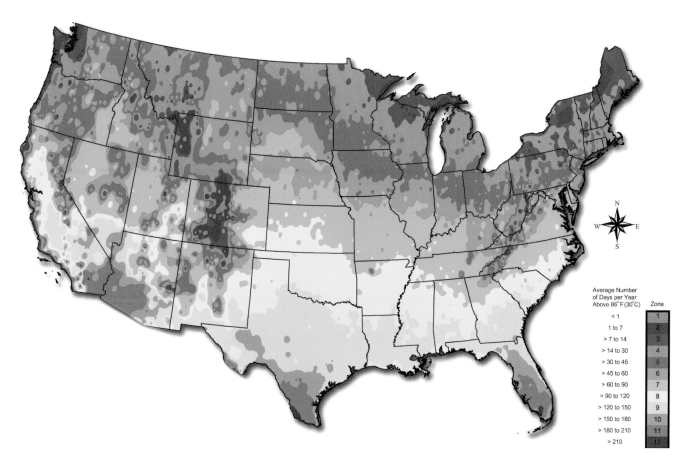

Average Number of Days per Year Above 86°F (30°C)	Zone
< 1	1
1 to 7	2
> 7 to 14	3
> 14 to 30	4
> 30 to 45	5
> 45 to 60	6
> 60 to 90	7
> 90 to 120	8
> 120 to 150	9
> 150 to 180	10
> 180 to 210	11
> 210	12

The American Horticultural Society Heat-Zone Map divides the United States into 12 zones based on the average annual number of days a region's temperatures climb above 86°F (30°C), the temperature at which the cellular proteins of plants begin to experience injury. Introduced in 1998, the AHS Heat-Zone Map holds significance, especially for gardeners in southern and transitional zones. Nurseries, growers, and other plant sources will gradually begin listing both cold hardiness and heat tolerance zones for plants, including grass plants. Using the USDA Plant Hardiness map, which can help determine a plant's cold tolerance, and the AHS Heat-Zone Map, gardeners will be able to safely choose plants that tolerate their region's lowest and highest temperatures.

Canada's Plant Hardiness Zone Map outlines the different zones in Canada where various types of trees, shrubs, and flowers will most likely survive. It is based on the average climatic conditions of each area. The hardiness map is divided into nine major zones: the harshest is 0 and the mildest is 8. Relatively few plants are suited to zone 0. Subzones (e.g., 4a or 4b, 5a or 5b) are also noted in the map legend. These subzones are most familiar to Canadian gardeners. Some significant local factors, such as micro-topography, amount of shelter, and subtle local variations in snow cover, are too small to be captured on the map. Year-to-year variations in weather and gardening techniques can also have a significant impact on plant survival in any particular location.

glossary

Acid soil A soil that tests lower than 7.0 on the pH scale.

Alkaline soil A soil that tests higher than 7.0 on the pH scale.

Amendments Organic or inorganic materials that improve soil structure, drainage, and nutrient-holding capacity. Some add nutrients.

Annual A plant that completes its entire life cycle in one growing season.

Axil The upper angle between a main stem and its branches or leaf petioles.

Basal plate The flat structure at the bottom of a bulb from which the roots grow.

Biennial A plant that completes its life cycle in two years. Most biennials form a rosette of leaves the first year and a flower stalk the second.

Bract A modified leaf that sometimes looks like a flower petal.

Bud An embryonic flower, leaf, or stem. Buds form on stems or plant crowns.

Bulb A fleshy underground structure that stores nutrients during a plant's annual dormant period. A true bulb is a modified flower bud or shoot enclosed in scales, or enlarged overlapping modified leaves. Other types of underground storage structures—tubers, tuberous roots, corms, and rhizomes—are often referred to as bulbs.

Bulb pan A wide shallow pan or pot used for forcing spring bulbs.

Calyx The protective modified leaves, or sepals, that surround the base of a flower.

Compound leaf A leaf that is divided into two or more distinct leaflets.

Corm The underground, swollen base of a stem from which new shoots and roots can grow. Crocuses grow from corms.

Corolla The group of petals that form a flower.

Corona The central cup- or tube-shaped part of a flower such as a daffodil.

Cotyledon The first leaf or set of leaves that a plant grows; these are also called seed leaves.

Crown The part of the plant where roots and stem meet, generally just below or at the soil line.

Cultivar Short for cultivated variety. Rather than occurring naturally in the wild, cultivars are developed. Cultivar names are enclosed in single quotes.

Cutting A piece of stem or root that is removed from a plant and used to propagate a new plant.

Deadheading Removing flowers after they have faded. Some plants prolong their bloom time when deadheaded.

Disbudding Removing some flower buds to promote larger flowers from remaining buds.

Disk flowers The small flowers in the center of a composite flower head such as a sunflower or daisy.

Division A propagation method that separates a plant into two or more pieces, each with at least one bud and some roots.

Foliar feeding To spray a plant's leaves with a fertilizer containing immediately available nutrients.

Forcing Causing a plant to flower indoors ahead of its natural blooming time.

Full shade Refers to a site that receives no direct sunlight.

Full sun Refers to a site that receives six or more hours a day of direct sunlight.

Genus (plural: genera) A closely related group of species that share similar characteristics. Genus names are italicized and capitalized.

Harden off To gradually acclimate a seedling started indoors to the harsher outdoor environment.

Hardiness A plant's ability to survive the climate in an area without protection from winter cold or summer heat, often described in relation to official Hardiness Zones.

Hardy annual An annual that can tolerate cool temperatures. Some hardy annuals tolerate freezing temperatures for short periods of time.

Herbaceous Plants whose stems and leaves die back to the ground each winter are herbaceous rather than woody.

Humus A material derived from the almost completely decomposed remains of organic matter. Highly complex in make-up, humus buffers soil acidity and alkalinity, holds water and nutrients, improves soil aggregation and structure, and contains many compounds that enhance plant growth.

Hybrid A plant resulting from cross breeding parent plants that belong to different varieties or cultivars, species, or sometimes even genera. Hybrids can be indicated by a times sign (×) between the genus and species name or the designation F1 or F2.

Inflorescence Any sort of flower cluster on a common stem. Sometimes used to refer to a single flower.

Invasive A plant that spreads easily and thus "invades" adjacent areas.

Leaflet One of the divisions on a compound leaf.

Microclimate Conditions of sun, shade, exposure, wind, drainage, and other factors at a particular site.

Mulch A covering on the soil. Mulches can be inorganic, as in plastic films, or organic, as in straw, chipped leaves, or shredded bark.

Node The point along a stem from which a leaf or roots emerge.

Offset A new plant that forms vegetatively; it usually grows at the base of the parent plant.

Perennial A plant that normally lives for three or more years.

Pesticide A substance that kills insect pests. The term is also used to describe other agricultural toxins, including fungicides and herbicides.

Petiole The stem of a leaf.

pH A measure of acidity or alkalinity. The pH scale runs from 0 to 14, where 7 represents neutral, numbers higher than 7 represent alkalinity and those lower than 7 represent acidity.

Plant habit The form a plant naturally takes as it grows, such as spreading, columnar, or rounded.

Propagate To create more plants. Plants also reproduce, or propagate, themselves.

Ray flowers The flowers surrounding the central disk in a composite flower.

Rhizome A creeping, often enlarged, stem that lies at or just under the soil surface. Both shoots and roots can form at nodes along the rhizome.

Rosette A low-growing, generally circular cluster of leaves that arises from a plant's crown.

Runner A low-growing stem that arises from the crown and runs along the ground. Runners can root at every node.

Seed leaf The first leaf or set of leaves produced by the embryo of a plant during its germination period. Also called a cotyledon.

Self-cleaning A term used to describe a plant that does not require deadheading. Spent flowers drop off by themselves and the plant continues to make new blooms.

Species A group of plants that shares many characteristics and can interbreed freely. The species name follows the genus name, is italicized, and is not capitalized.

Succulent Fleshy, water-filled plant tissues. Plants with tissues like these are often referred to as a succulent.

Tender perennial A plant that is perennial in frost-free environments but dies when exposed to freezing temperatures.

True leaf The second and subsequent leaves or sets of leaves that a plant produces. The first leaf or set of leaves are seed leaves, or cotyledons. True leaves have the distinctive shape of the leaves of the mature plant.

Tuber A swollen stem that grows underground. Both roots and shoots grow from tubers.

Tuberous roots Enlarged roots that have growth buds at the crown (the area where the plant's roots meet the stems).

Variegated Foliage that is marked, striped, or blotched with a color other than the basic green of the leaf.

Whorl Leaves or petals growing in a circular cluster around a stem.

index

Glossary/Index

index

photo credits

All photos by David Cavagnaro unless otherwise noted.

page 3: *middle left* Positive Images *bottom left* John Glover **page 5:** both *right* John Glover **page 6:** *left* John Glover *top right* Alan *and* Linda Detrick **page 7:** *top* Charles Mann *bottom* Walter Chandoha **page 13:** Grant Heilman/Lefever/Grushow **page 14:** *top left* John Glover *bottom left* Rick Mastelli *bottom right* Bruce Coleman **page 15:** *left* Charles Mann **page 16:** *top left* Derek Fell **page 18:** *left* Derek Fell **page 20:** *left* Michael Thompson **page 21:** *top right* Jerry Pavia *bottom right* Derek Fell **page 22:** *top left* John Glover *top right* John Glover **page 23:** *both top* John Glover *both bottom* Neil Soderstrom **page 26:** *left* Virginia Weinland **page 27:** *top and bottom left* Derek Fell *bottom middle* Liz Ball **page 30:** *left* Rod Cardillo *both right* Jerry Pavia **page 32:** *top and bottom left* John Glover *bottom left* Jerry Pavia **page 33:** *top left* Ben Phillips/Positive Images *top right* John Glover *bottom left and right* John Glover *bottom middle* Positive Images **page 35:** *top left* John Glover *bottom right* The Garden Picture Library **page 36:** *middle* John Glover *bottom* The Garden Picture Library **page 37:** *top* Michael Thompson **page 39:** *top* John Glover *bottom right* Sunniva Harte/Garden Picture Library **page 40:** *both right* Neil Soderstrom **page 41:** *right* Charles Mann **page 44:** *left* John Glover **page 45:** *top right and bottom left* John Glover **page 47:** *top* Positive Images **page 48:** *bottom right* Howard Rice **page 51:** *top* Jerry Pavia *inset* E.R. Degginger **page 53:** *top middle* Positive Images *bottom* Neil Soderstrom **page 54:** *top* John Glover *bottom* Derek Fell **page 55:** *left and top*

right Jerry Pavia **page 57:** *left* E.R. Degginger *middle* Photo Researchers, Inc. *right* Rob Cardillo **page 58:** *bottom left and middle* Neil Soderstrom **page 60:** *bottom left and middle* Neil Soderstrom *bottom right* Photo Researchers, Inc. **page 61:** *top* Liz Ball *bottom left* Photo Researchers, Inc. **page 62:** *left* John Glover *top and middle right* Liz Ball *bottom right* Jerry Pavia **page 64:** *top left* Neil Soderstrom *top right* Positive Images *bottom right* Neil Soderstrom **page 65:** *top* Neil Soderstrom *bottom left* Alan *and* Linda Detrick *bottom middle* Derek Fell **page 66:** *right* Positive Images *inset* John Glover **page 67:** *top left* Liz Ball *top right* Neil Soderstrom *bottom left* Derek Fell *bottom right* Charles Mann **page 69:** *top* Positive Images *middle* John Glover *bottom right* Jerry Pavia **page 70:** *left* Positive Images *bottom left* John Glover *bottom right* Netherland Flower Bulb Information Center **page 71:** John Glover **page 73:** Neil Soderstrom **page 74:** *left* Neil Soderstrom *right* Michael Thompson **page 75:** *right and inset* John Glover **page 79:** *top right* Ben Phillips/Positive Images **page 80:** *both top and bottom left* Alan *and* Linda Detrick *both right* Alan *and* Linda Detrick **page 81:** *bottom left* Neil Soderstrom **page 82:** *left* Michael Thompson *right* Lamontagne/The Garden Picture Library **page 83:** *left* John Glover **page 84:** *top left* J.S. Sira/ The Garden Picture Library *top right* Jerry Pavia *bottom left* Howard Rice/The Garden Picture Library *bottom right* Neil Soderstrom **page 86:** *right* Neil Soderstrom **page 89:** John Glover **page 90:** *top* John Glover

All illustrations by Mavis Torke.